POWER
Listening

POWER
Listening

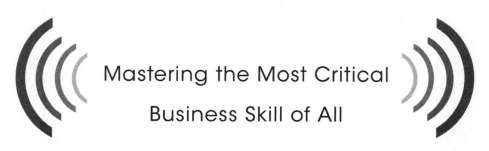

Mastering the Most Critical

Business Skill of All

Bernard T. Ferrari

PORTFOLIO/PENGUIN

PORTFOLIO / PENGUIN
Published by the Penguin Group
Penguin Group (USA) Inc., 375 Hudson Street,
New York, New York 10014, U.S.A.
Penguin Group (Canada), 90 Eglinton Avenue East, Suite 700, Toronto, Ontario,
Canada M4P 2Y3 (a division of Pearson Penguin Canada Inc.)
Penguin Books Ltd, 80 Strand, London WC2R 0RL, England
Penguin Ireland, 25 St. Stephen's Green, Dublin 2, Ireland
(a division of Penguin Books Ltd)
Penguin Books Australia Ltd, 250 Camberwell Road, Camberwell, Victoria 3124,
Australia (a division of Pearson Australia Group Pty Ltd)
Penguin Books India Pvt Ltd, 11 Community Centre, Panchsheel Park,
New Delhi – 110 017, India
Penguin Group (NZ), 67 Apollo Drive, Rosedale, Auckland 0632,
New Zealand (a division of Pearson New Zealand Ltd)
Penguin Books (South Africa) (Pty) Ltd, 24 Sturdee Avenue,
Rosebank, Johannesburg 2196, South Africa

Penguin Books Ltd, Registered Offices:
80 Strand, London WC2R 0RL, England

First published in 2012 by Portfolio / Penguin,
a member of Penguin Group (USA) Inc.

3   5   7   9   10   8   6   4   2

LIBRARY OF CONGRESS CATALOGING IN PUBLICATION DATA

Ferrari, Bernard T.
Power listening : mastering the most critical business skill of all / Bernard T. Ferrari.
p.   cm.
Includes index.
ISBN 978-1-59184-462-4
1. Business communication.   2. Listening.   I. Title.
HF5718.F48 2012
658.4'5—dc23
2011037614

Printed in the United States of America
Set in Baskerville
Designed by Jaime Putorti

Dedicated to the first listeners
in my life, my parents.

AUTHOR'S NOTE AND ACKNOWLEDGMENTS

When I first contemplated this book, I asked myself if anyone would really be interested in reading about listening for the purpose of arriving at a better business decision. My question stemmed from a comment made to me years ago by an executive, who said, "No one in business listens! They don't see any need to." The longer I thought about that comment the more misguided this attitude seemed to be, and the more convinced I became that I should tackle the subject. For starters, I realized that the greatest business managers I've encountered show an uncanny ability to listen. Further, I couldn't deny the fact that I had derived my own way of listening by observing the many talented executives whom I had the privilege to advise, as well as those McKinsey & Company colleagues who demonstrated their own great listening skills over the twenty years I was part of "the Firm." Fortified by the conviction that good listening figures centrally in business performance, and that my goal was to pass on a collected set of lessons, I began to write.

Still, something was missing. I grew concerned that perhaps the executives who constituted my research sample group were tainted by some selection bias. They were all my clients, after all. So in hopes of sidestepping that particular trap, I asked many of McKinsey's current partners to nominate the best business listeners they had encountered, for additional interview subjects. To my relief and my delight, virtually everything I heard in this new round of interviews confirmed and reinforced what I had learned from my clients.

I had two considerations in writing this book, beyond the subject itself. The first was to make the book as applicable to the beginning manager or business decision maker as to the more seasoned executive. The second was to be respectful of the reader's time. I have been as economical in my prose as my ability allows, while still getting across everything I believe to be relevant.

I also want to make the important point that gender offers no advantage or disadvantage to listening in the workplace. I ask you to bear this in mind whenever you come across the use of the masculine pronoun in this book, when a construction like "he or she" or "him or her" might feel more correct. I have used the masculine pronoun only to simplify the style and presentation of the book.

In my service to my clients, I always considered myself a guest in their companies, and always had a professional and legal obligation to keep their confidences. When they gave me permission to tell their stories, I have used their names. When they were shy about doing so or when I used individuals' stories as examples of what not to do, I changed the situations and the industries in question so they would be unidentifiable, perhaps even to the subjects themselves.

I have been fortunate to have a great deal of support in writing this book. I must acknowledge Jeffrey Immelt, who encouraged me and graciously wrote the foreword. My friends and colleagues at McKinsey & Company, who identified the great listeners and taught me much of what I share with you, are too numerous to thank individually. They know who they are, and I thank each of them for their generosity and partnership. A few played a special role, including Dominic Barton, Michael Patsalos-Fox, Ted Hall, the late Roger Kline, Larry Kanarek, Vik Malhotra, and Pete Walker.

I had the good fortune to observe a number of great listeners during one of my earlier lives, in medicine. The late Dr. George Engel, as a professor of psychiatry at the University of Rochester, provided me and my fellow medical students our first lessons in listening. He once told me that I had a lot of work to do to be a perceptive physician, but added that he had faith in me. He was right about the work to be done, and I very much hope that he would approve of this effort. Another mentor was the late Dr. William Longmire, a professor and the chairman of surgery at UCLA. He was one of those rare individuals who, after a brief conversation in which he would ask a few key questions, would appear to know your mind. And I want to send my apologies to Dr. Frank Riddick, who gave me my first managerial job at the Ochsner Clinic in New Orleans, Louisiana, and who knew better than anyone how bad a listener I was. Thank you, Frank, for never giving up on me.

I warmly thank Killian Clarke, my trusted and valuable research assistant, for his work on this project. Without Killian there would be no book. Jessica Goethals ensured that we got our medieval and Renaissance facts right. Others at Ferrari Consultancy who provided support were Todd Johnson, Patrick Sullivan, and Sherry Babb. David Sobel was a great help, providing valuable editorial support. Many times, when I found myself tongue-tied, David was able to loosen the knots. Jim Levine, my literary agent, and William Hart, my attorney, provided great guidance and encouragement. The professionals at Portfolio, including my talented editor, Jillian Gray; one of the wise men of publishing, Adrian Zackheim; and the great marketing and publicity team, Will Weisser, Allison McLean, and

Tiffany Liao, got this work over the finish line with minimal pain to the author.

Lastly, I must thank the one individual who I believe is the greatest listener of all, my wife, Linda. For nearly forty years she has been listening to me, and, for reasons I can't quite fathom, she has remained interested in what I have to say. For that I am truly grateful.

FOREWORD

When I catalog the traits and practices that I want to emphasize in General Electric, and that I strive to improve in myself, the first item on my list is to become a better listener. If you're like I was, you've probably never thought very carefully about listening before; but I've realized that listening isn't some natural gift like athletic ability or an ear for music. It's a skill that demands conscious attention and constant practice, because only through good listening can any of us gather the information we need to do our jobs well.

I recall reading Antony Beevor's book *D-Day: The Battle for Normandy*, in which he described Dwight Eisenhower as being a great leader largely because he was such a good listener. The general never shut out any individual's voice, and by the same token, no one escaped his careful probing and questioning. When the time came, he was prepared to make the tough decisions. That characterization has stuck with me; Eisenhower's leadership never depended on fear or intimidation, but rather was founded on the trust and respect he demonstrated through engaged and attentive listening.

How well are you listening? I ask myself the question all the time. Do I honestly engage with people whose opinions differ from mine? Am I ready and willing to accept critical inputs? I believe that successful twenty-first-century leaders will have to be humble listeners. They will seek out and gather information from many sources, and use those inputs to catalyze new ways of thinking and generate new insights. They will understand that asking many questions is more useful to an organization than finding quick answers and handy solutions. They will not only welcome debate, they will demand it from everyone around them.

I've worked with Bernie Ferrari for many years now. We have grown, and become better listeners, together. I've come to count on Bernie to use the techniques he describes in this book to change the refraction of a problem, so that together, we can hope to arrive at fresh insights and solutions. We've internalized these techniques to the point where we try to ensure that neither of us misses any important point, or fails to ask a critical question, when analyzing problems or making decisions for the future. I believe that I have become more valuable to my company as a result.

Listening may be the single most undervalued and undeveloped business skill, especially in an age of increasing uncertainty and fast-paced change. Bernie Ferrari's book comes along just in time, offering insights that enable any individual to sharpen their listening, and in so doing, contribute to the improved performance of their organization. I hope you can take on board what Bernie has to teach. I can tell you from experience that the rewards will be plentiful.

JEFFREY R. IMMELT

CHAIRMAN AND CEO, GENERAL ELECTRIC COMPANY

CONTENTS

CONTENTS

(((Reaping the Benefits)))

POWER
Listening

Listen Up!

It was an uncomfortable meeting.

"Why didn't anyone see this coming?" asked the CEO. "Why weren't we prepared for this possibility?"

I was watching from the corner of a conference room. The CEO had asked me to sit in and observe, so that I could start to put together an assessment of how his management team was making decisions. He was asking some tough questions about a failed introduction of a product into a new market. The CEO wanted some answers from his team.

The room grew quiet and tense. I could see some team members shooting each other furtive looks. Finally, one woman bravely spoke up.

"You know," she ventured, "we tried to tell you a number of times. We were never quite sure you were listening."

I realized, at that moment, that my assessment of his team would have to start at the top.

This CEO had received one of the most common pieces of

upward and downward feedback passed along in the world of business, one that very few businesspeople manage to avoid. Leaders at all levels and in myriad positions are told that they could be better listeners. If you are one of those managers who has been told in the past that you need to listen better, or you have become aware that you are not making enough good business decisions, then what I have to say should interest you. Indeed, the question my client later posed to me—What am I supposed to do with these suggestions about being a better listener?—is one that many ask, but few know how to answer. And yet, learning how to answer this question is critical to success in business.

Listening can well be the difference between profit and loss, between success and failure, between a long career and a short one. Listening is the only way to find out what you don't know, and marks the path to making good decisions, arriving at the best ideas. If you aspire to be better at your job, no matter what it is, listening may be the most powerful tool at your disposal.

I have lived four professional lives: surgeon, lawyer, businessman, and consultant. Though each career had its own unique domain knowledge, they all had something in common. The leaders in each field—those most respected, accomplished, and able to inspire others—outdistanced their peers by practicing better listening skills. I began my career as a surgeon, which may explain why some of my colleagues and clients say that I have a more clinical method of listening than most consultants. While the doctor-patient relationship is far different from what you'll find in business, one broadly applicable thing I learned in medicine is that you have to ask a lot of direct questions to really understand what's being said and why it's being said. Since every patient is unique, and each illness or injury manifests itself differently from patient to patient, asking the right questions, and listening carefully to the answers, were the keys not only to making a good diagnosis, but also to managing treatment. Later, those skills helped me understand and address issues in the clinic I helped manage, and in the organizations and corporations to which I consulted.

The listening techniques I started using as a physician have served me well through all my professional incarnations. I ask pesky questions, but if at the end of the day those managers with whom I work have had to challenge their assumptions and open their minds to new aspects of a business issue, then that's a win for everyone.

My time as a physician helped me learn some key listening techniques. However, the majority of this book is based on my experiences working as a consultant to CEOs and high-level managers in some of the world's largest companies and nonprofit organizations. My work with these leaders has given me a unique vantage point from which to observe who wins and who loses—and why. Over time I became convinced that winning, both individually and organizationally, depended on a superior ability to listen. The truly outstanding managers I observed had each figured out for him or herself how to master this skill. I've taken the best of their techniques and distilled them into a form that I hope will be the easiest and most fruitful for you. They listened well to their colleagues, their customers, their regulators, their suppliers, and sometimes even their competitors. The lessons I learned from them are the lessons I pass on in this book. I should add that they are lessons that I myself have had to learn. I know what it's like to go from poor listening to better listening. This means I also know that it can be learned, practiced, and improved. Though the process can be frustrating at times, I can say from experience that becoming a better listener is not only possible, but it can also have an incredible impact on you and your organization's performance.

When I finally came to realize that the difference between great and mediocre managers was the ability to listen, I began searching for business experts who had written on listening. It was a relatively fruitless search. I found that an awful lot of lip service is paid to the need for better communication, but experts were only addressing one side of the equation. According to the American Society for Training and Development, U.S. businesses and organizations spend a total of well over $100 billion each year developing the skills of their workers. An estimated 20 percent of that vast sum goes to communications courses. Of the nearly three hundred communications courses offered by the American Management Association, only two deal directly with listening skills. I have to wonder how valuable it is to have all those well-trained business writers and public speakers and skilled presenters if their audiences aren't equally skilled at listening.

The old adage that it is better to give than to receive breaks down when it comes to business communication and decision making. There are steps you can take that can turn even a *tin ear* into a *platinum ear*, a precious asset for any manager. Turning tin into platinum in this way is not some fanciful alchemy. We can actually achieve this kind of transformation in our listening skills. Listening is no more a passive, innate ability than speaking is. If we can teach people to write and speak more clearly or more persuasively, if we can break down the process of imparting information into discrete, *learnable* steps, then we can do the same with the process of receiving information.

Of course, some people are better writers than others, and we can't all be Shakespeare or Jefferson. The same holds true for listening, which like any other human endeavor is a combination of art and science, of nature and nurture, or of instinct and calculation. Some people are more naturally empathetic, and can read unspoken clues more easily. Some people have sharper analytical skills, or more highly developed critical thinking. However, by recognizing where our individual strengths and weaknesses lie, and by adopting a set of straightforward, proactive listening techniques, anyone can sharpen their ears and take a step closer to making better decisions.

Like anyone who writes about business skills, my goal is to improve business performance. In this book, I've tried to lay out a relatively straightforward path that enables us to move quickly from better insight to more focused and effective action. In the first of three main sections, I'll run through the fundamentals of thoughtful, directed listening that will improve your chances of taking in all the information you'll need to make decisions and set your course of action. Here we'll take a quick look at some of the common misconceptions about good listening, and I'll describe a few general types of listeners that I've identified over the years. The better we understand the predictable mistakes made by each type of listener, and the more we recognize the telltale characteristics in ourselves, the easier it will be to address our own individual listening shortcomings.

Once we've established common pitfalls, and outlined some ways to avoid them, I'll walk you through what I believe are the basic principles of good listening. First, I'll talk about respect. Managers often fall into predictable patterns of interaction with the people around them, and can develop a complacency about these routines that can hinder productive communication. The best managers, however, are always on the alert, believing that valuable insights may lurk in the unlikeliest places. Take nothing that you hear for granted, and try to sustain respect for the ideas of each of your colleagues. The next step may seem obvious: Keep quiet! You have to get out of the way of the conversation in order to hear what's important. This isn't the time to seek the spotlight or to prove your own smarts. You don't need to keep stonily silent, but you should speak only to help bring out your conversation partner's points. (Throughout this book I use the expression "conversation partner" or "CP" to refer to the person with whom you are communicating.)

Next, I'll talk about assumptions, which I consider to be among the biggest obstacles to good listening. Holding on to entrenched assumptions will make you deaf; by allowing your assumptions to be challenged you render yourself more prepared to be surprised and more flexible in your business actions and decisions. Finally, I'll introduce some techniques to help you keep your mind in the game and focused on what's important. Buddhists sometimes talk about *mindfulness*, a state in which you completely empty your mind but at the same time try to step outside the experience so that you can observe, analyze, and comprehend it intellectually. A good listener must do the same: clear your mind of preconceptions, unrelated enmities, pet peeves, and hobbyhorses so that you can be open to fresh ideas and at the same time keep your critical-thinking skills finely tuned and constantly on alert.

If we listen well in business, our minds will quickly become filled with layer upon layer of information and ideas. What do we do with all these data? And what exactly should we be listening for? In the second section, I'll talk about how to organize this chaos. I admit that listening to conversations is messy, but it is possible for you to impose order. We all know the importance of organizing information into good files, whether we were raised on manila folders and clanging steel cabinets or carry a virtual desktop around on our laptops or smartphones. The key to good listening is to develop a filing system in our heads, and to ask questions that get those folders and cabinets adequately filled. I devote a chapter to each of the following categories, which represent the labels on the file cabinets I use to help me sort out my listening.

▶ *Get to the mandate.* Sometimes simply getting clarity on the specific dream, aspiration, or organizational mission underlying the discussion can make all the difference.

▶ *Understand the plan.* How are we going to get from A to B? We have to understand each individual step if we want to be able to navigate toward a successful outcome.

▶ *Know who is on the team.* Is this discussion about people and how they will work together?

▶ *Be aware of how well you are executing.* Build your understanding around the risks and rewards, measurements, and accountability that will drive effective execution of the plan.

▶ *Be mindful of the personal.* People are not automatons. Character and personality traits can impact what information is being offered.

The third and last section is about getting to action. In the end, we listen because we have to make tough calls that affect our business. Here, I talk about what to *do* with all the necessary information you gather and sort using the techniques from the first two sections of the book. I believe that listening drives performance, both in yourself and in an entire organization. So I begin by talking about how better listening can improve your judgment and help you make better decisions. Then I move on to discuss collective performance, and how your good listening will actually raise the game of your entire organization. The habits you develop as you hone your listening skills will spill over into all areas of your organization, changing the culture and raising the levels of focus, efficiency, candor, creativity, and respect.

All the accomplished business leaders I've ever known strive to improve the quality of their decisions and to raise their organization's performance. Good listening can be transformative to both those ends. Regardless of whether you have a staff of two or you're managing a global workforce of a hundred thousand, you can use focused and targeted listening to bring the best ideas out of the people in your organization, leading each individual to fresh insight that can, in turn, drive better actions and become the engine of your success.

SECTION
ONE

(((1)))

Listening Is Worth the Effort

When someone tells me about a meeting they've attended, or recounts a conversation they've had, they'll often say something like, "At that point, I stopped talking for a moment. It was good to catch my breath and rest for a bit." It's an interesting comment, because it creates the impression that *talking* involves more effort than *listening*. In fact, just the opposite should be true. I believe that good listening burns more calories than talking ever will. Furthermore, I'm convinced that this misperception—that listening is somehow equivalent to resting—leads people to believe that listening is a passive rather than an active endeavor. From that false premise naturally flows the assumption that listening can be a time waster, rather than an effective means of advancing the ball.

Understand that the kind of listening I'm talking about here differs greatly from what you might do, for instance, at a music concert. I'm not talking about being a member of the audience. I'm talking about being a participant in a conversation even while remaining silent. Think about looking at a painting in an art museum.

A painting is the creation of another person, a fact that in and of itself demands intellectual engagement from the viewer. A guide at the Metropolitan Museum of Art in New York once described to me how visitors from around the world will approach her with a slightly intimidated look on their faces, and ask, basically, how to look at a particular work of art. She'll walk them over to a painting and take them through a series of questions about the choices the artist has made—about light and color, angles and perspective, technique and composition—that open up a new world of understanding for the viewer. The answers to these questions, or sometimes merely the exercise of formulating the questions, can reveal the artistic intent behind the work.

Apply this idea to listening and you'll see what I mean about focused, *active* listening. There are four major reasons I view good listening in the business setting as a critical activity, and a strenuous one at that.

1. *Listening is purposeful.* A disciplined businessperson enters a conversation with a clear understanding of what it needs to accomplish.

2. *Listening requires control.* Even when you're on the receiving end of a communication, you need to steer and filter the incoming information in order to accomplish your purpose.

3. *Listening requires total focus and engagement.* When you listen with intent, you must bring a heightened awareness to the conversation, so that you can formulate the right questions and generate the necessary interjections and interruptions (a subject I'll talk about in more depth later) to advance the conversation productively.

LISTENING IS WORTH THE EFFORT

4. *Listening is the front end of decision making.* It's the surest, most efficient route to informing the judgments you will need to make.

Let me tell you about a top executive, a leader of one of America's largest companies, with whom I've met every month or so over many years. He would begin almost every conversation with the same simple query: "How do you see the world?" It was practically a reflex for him; it almost seemed that the question would be out of his mouth before the "lo" in "hello." The executive accomplished quite a lot with that little opening gambit. First, he established that it was time to talk business. I always understood this short question as a signal that, although this client and I knew each other fairly well, this was not the time to talk about summer vacations, or anything personal for that matter. What my client wanted from me was some insight about the world *as it was relevant to his business.*

Second, it represented something of a test, as when a pitcher throws something high and inside to see if the batter will flinch, or foul it off, or maybe even slap it up the middle. You could say he was qualifying me as his conversation partner, gauging my level of engagement. This test takes on different characteristics depending on the relationship between the conversation partners. Before we really knew much about each other, the executive would find in my response clues to what kind of listener I was. From there, he could extrapolate an idea of how I thought and how I processed ideas and information. How one listens can be a sophisticated indicator of one's approach to thinking and one's overall capability. Later, after we became more familiar with each other, he could determine where I was on that particular day. Was I bringing my "A game"? Was I distracted or engaged? Did I take the subject at hand seriously enough?

Third, he was subtly taking control of the conversation by asking the questions that would move it in the direction he needed to go. Conversely, he could show that I had permission to tell him what I needed out of the conversation, and then let me know if he had time for, and interest in, my agenda.

Initially, I would give a pretty straightforward answer to this rhetorical question, actually offering whatever insight I could come up with about the world. Over the years, as we got to know each other and I became a better listener as well as a better communicator, I learned to answer the question in such a way as to move the conversation toward my agenda. The client and I would go through a little back-and-forth until we each had a sense of what the other needed from the conversation. Naturally, that process became more streamlined the longer we worked together.

His agendas were fairly complex, mirroring the enormous complexity of a multifaceted organization operating across an ever-shifting global economic landscape. Amazingly, our conversations rarely lasted more than an hour. Our discussions were crisp, efficient, and peppered with pointed questions from both of us.

After all, it's always about time in the end, isn't it? I'm constantly amazed by businesspeople of all stripes who grouse about their chock-a-block schedules and unmanageable commitments. In truth, I lament their careers, and in particular, I'm both saddened and frustrated that these people use these pressures almost to excuse their lack of attention to better listening. The true stars, the busiest and most heavily committed of this group, never appear hassled or harried. It might be going too far to describe their style as casual, but they do not appear rushed. They appear deliberate, taking as much time as they need, *but no more*, to gather information, through practiced probing, questioning, steering, and editing each conversation and interaction. I often marvel at how these busy leaders can maneuver a conversation, or even cut it off completely, without appearing rude or disrespectful.

In an extreme example of the crafted conversation for purposeful listening, another executive I knew would line up back-to-back phone calls with other high-powered executives, so he could move smoothly and efficiently through them. Not a moment would be wasted no matter who was on the phone, whether a high-level government official or another CEO. The more highly placed the conversation partner, the more likely that he or she would value the focused, disciplined conversation as much as he did.

I hope my point is obvious: You can't think of careful listening as something that *takes* time. On the contrary, good listening *buys* time. This point was hit home for me when John McLaughlin, the former Deputy Director of the CIA, described to me the greatest challenge that leaders face: "We get ambiguous, incomplete, imperfect information arriving incrementally . . . and you're being pressured to act." That is the challenge, and in many ways listening is the solution. Listening well means bringing discipline and control to your conversations, which helps you to sort through all the messy information. It means getting what you need from each exchange more quickly, as well as allowing you to ensure that your conversation partner gets what he or she needs. Moreover, it frees up time, because you don't have to keep rehashing the same conversations, and when you *do* act the calls you make will be better. Nothing wastes more time in the business world than a series of bad decisions.

The frenzied executive who always seems to be running around with his hair on fire, drowning under the information swirling around him, has issues that go well beyond time management. To my mind, that manager is as good as finished, whether or not he realizes it. He is someone who has let go of the reins and allowed himself to be swept up by circumstances. It goes without saying that no manager can be successful while allowing himself to be buffeted by external forces.

Ironically, these are the people who most often say that they don't have the time to devote to better listening. They could not be more wrong. Kevin Sharer, the CEO of the biopharmaceutical company Amgen, has a theory that high-level executives tend to burn out because they fail to develop good listening skills. In his opinion, listening helps him to operate more efficiently and create more available time in his days. In this sense, he says that listening has a "sparing effect" on his managerial routine, allowing him to operate with greater peace of mind and streamline his thinking so that he doesn't get driven to distraction.

Highly developed listening skills increase your focus and your sense of control. You will see the change in your own performance and productivity. More important, good listening skills will enable you to bring forth more fully developed ideas from the people around you. In the best of all worlds, it can facilitate streamlined analysis, more focused planning, and more sure-handed decision making.

The most exciting part is that, once you get good at listening, you will be able to do it easily, almost effortlessly, without even thinking about it. The techniques I propose will perhaps seem overly deliberate and cumbersome to work through in practice. They may be at first, and you may get frustrated. But just like any other skill they will become second nature with time. In David Brooks's book *The Social Animal: The Hidden Sources of Love, Character, and Achievement* he describes a line of cognitive research that examines how star athletes' brains work when they are running, hitting, shooting, or passing. The research finds that during these moments athletes' brains are actually quieter than nonathletes' brains as they engage in the same physical activities. The athletes have trained themselves so well they don't have to expend mental energy on thinking about what they're doing. The movement, actions, decisions, reactions become intuitive. Scientists showed a group of basketball players and nonbasketball players the same film clips of free throws, but without revealing whether the shots went in. The basketball players were far superior at predicting whether the free throws were successful, simply because they could sense intuitively whether the shooters had the right torque, speed, and motion.

In my experience, becoming a good listener happens in precisely the same way. At first it will seem difficult to train yourself in this new set of skills. The process we'll undertake together is analogous to anything from learning a new aria or a concerto to rebuilding a golf swing to developing a reliable free throw. You need to break an activity down into its smallest component parts, and then examine, analyze, and repair each one of those parts before reassembling it all into a seamless whole. I'm not saying it's easy, but I know it's worth the effort. Stick with me, and with time I have faith that you'll be shooting listening free throws just like the pros. Your mind will be calm, your instincts will take hold, and you will be surprised by how efficient and productive you become.

(((2)))

What Kind of Listener Are You?

On the day I graduated from medical school, I raised my right hand to take the Hippocratic Oath and recited those very important words "do no harm." As I went on in my medical career, I learned that the surest path to violating that oath, despite my best intentions, was to proceed with treatment under a misdiagnosis. As a former surgical mentor said to me again and again: "Can't fix it if you don't know what's wrong."

Those words are not unique to medicine. In business, the consequences of failing to properly frame or assess an issue can be dire. Often such a misdiagnosis in business is the result of not having the right information. Though the necessary information is often available, businesspeople sometimes don't know how to find it or don't see it in front of them. The reason: poor listening skills. To improve your listening skills, you must first figure out exactly what is keeping you from seeking and hearing the information you need. Are you hearing only what you want to hear? Are you answering only your own questions? Are you faking it? I'm going to describe six of the more common archetypes of bad listeners. I call these "archetypes" because no one is a pure case. Characteristic behaviors of each archetype can be demonstrated by a single individual at different times and under different circumstances. In fact, I admit that I've demonstrated all six, sometimes on the same day. My goal is to help you recognize the symptoms of these specific listening syndromes—and here is the tough part—so you can sense when you slip into these bad behaviors. You will be like a doctor turning the tools of diagnosis on yourself. If you can use these descriptions to set up some alarm bells for your own off-putting behavior, then we have taken the first step in curing what ails you.

Many men and women who have risen to the top of an organization have convinced themselves that they owe their success to an unwavering faith in their own personal vision and judgment, or their ability to see clearly through the fog of conflicting information all around them. I knew one CEO of a major industrial company, a seasoned executive, who had a habit of cutting people off three sentences into the presentation of a new idea. "Look," he would snap, "let me tell you how I see this . . ." From there, he would proceed to express his opinion with no uncertainty. This CEO was a classic example of the first type of poor listener I want to discuss: the **Opinionator**. At the heart of an Opinionator's problem is his tendency to listen to others really only to determine whether or not his ideas conform to what the Opinionator already knows to be true. The Opinionator may believe that he is listening intently, and indeed he may very well be, but that doesn't mean he's listening with an open mind. This kind of listener probably has the best of intentions, but the net effect of this listening style is that conversation partners feel intimidated or at least somewhat uncomfortable, and colleagues' ideas—good or bad—are routinely squelched.

The Opinionator reminds me of the author and business-school professor Laurence Peter's quip, "When I want your opinion, I'll give it to you." A telltale sign of an Opinionator is the tendency to start sentences with "Listen . . ." and to end them with ". . . right?"

A second archetype of poor listening takes the Opinionator one step further. Whereas the Opinonator's listening is limited by his belief that his ideas are right, the **Grouch** is blocked by the certainty that your ideas are wrong. A typical Grouch, a top executive officer I worked with at an industrial corporation, made no secret of his contempt for other people's ideas. He approached any conversation as some kind of necessary evil, a painful, futile experience through which he'd have to suffer. This Grouch might express his displeasure differently to different people, but his responses all seemed to carry the same implicit message: "You're full of it. You're a fool. Why did you even think I'd be interested in this?"

I used to coach teams at his company to prepare them for dealing with him. The first fifteen minutes of the meeting will be hell, I told them, but if you press on bravely, he will eventually acknowledge you. It was true; by the end of many meetings, the Grouch would say, "OK. Yeah, I get it. I understand this now." It was, however, cold comfort to think that you might eventually get through to this man. I knew plenty of people in the company who just didn't have it in them to break through those barriers every time they needed to express an idea to him, and I worried about what it cost the company in missed opportunities over time.

In 2004, the television comedian Jon Stewart appeared as a guest on CNN's *Crossfire* program. Instead of engaging in the expected witty banter, Stewart confronted the two hosts, saying that the "debate" and "discourse" on the show was a sham, a theatrical device designed to let them vent their own political views. Television pundits have become the very embodiment of the poor-listening archetype I call the **Preambler.** The Preambler's windy lead-ins and questions are really stealth speeches, often designed to box his CP in. The Preambler uses this questioning technique to steer the conversation, or to send out a warning, or to produce a desired answer, as if the dialogue had been scripted.

My favorite example of a preamble moment was at a meeting I had with the board chairman and CEO of a medical complex. The CEO was making a recommendation to the board for a major and expensive shift in strategy. The chairman wanted another opinion. He invited me to a preliminary meeting with his CEO to see if I could help. I began by asking the CEO what question he thought we should be answering. By my watch, it took him fifteen minutes to get to the simple question "Are we making the right strategy decision?" He filled the elapsed time with slanted and rhetorical questions and assertions that would corner anyone into believing that his recommendation was the only one the board could follow. No wonder the chairman called me! Of course, the problem with speeches and loaded or rhetorical questions is that they are the very definition of one-way communication, and that's not very conducive to problem solving.

The **Perseverator** talks too much, in the way the Preambler does, but presents difficulties that are more subtle but no less confounding. The Perseverator may appear to be engaged in productive dialogue, but if you pay attention, you might notice that he's not really advancing the conversation. As often as not, he's actually editing on the fly, fine-tuning what he is saying through constant reiteration. His goal is not necessarily to sharpen the focus, but often only to help him sharpen his point or shoehorn your thoughts into supporting his prejudices and biases.

One executive I know has the habit of holding forth on an idea for a while, and then pausing, an apparent cue to start moving on to the next topic. Should you be so bold as to jump into that pause and try to move the discussion forward, he is likely to interrupt you with a couple more paragraphs along the same path he has just been following. It's as if you and he are having two completely different conversations.

Here is a sample from a conversation I had over dinner with a Perseverator. He had made the decision to move ahead with an acquisition, and was already through the first celebratory drink when I sat down.

> *Client:* I'm excited by the prospect of this acquisition. It's at an attractive price for us.
>
> *BTF:* How much thought have you given as to whether you can really develop its technologies?
>
> *Client:* Well, sure. It has great technologies and even greater potential. Plus, it's cheap.
>
> *BTF:* I ask my question because there are some important issues to consider. For instance, there is no significant overlap between your technology and its technology. And its development time is much shorter than what you are used to. And last, I wonder if you'll be able to hold on to its talent.
>
> *Client:* It's a steal at nine times earnings.
>
> *BTF:* Yes it is, if the technology is developed.
>
> *Client [after a long pause, which I mistakenly took as his deep thought about my question]:* And its balance sheet is pretty strong as well. Yeah, I like the price for all it brings us.

A Perseverator seems to be traveling the same worn mental path. He is fixated on, sometimes even obsessed with, a particular idea or set of ideas, and will remind you of that proverbial worker who possesses only a hammer, so that every challenge looks like a nail. The Perseverator may seem to be engaging in a dialogue, until you figure out that his statements not only don't advance the conversation, but may not even be directed at you. He is busy thinking out loud, and will eventually lead everyone back to the same predictable place.

Everyone likes to be the problem solver. You grab the spotlight and deliver what's needed to figure out a difficult problem or lay down the path to a required action. An extreme version of the problem solver reveals himself in conversation as the **Answer Man**. This is the person who starts spouting solutions before there is even a consensus about what the challenge might be, signaling that he is finished listening to your input in the conversation. On the surface, the Answer Man may seem quite similar to the Opinionator, but there is a fundamental difference. The Opinionator is hamstrung by the certainty that he or she is simply right, and probably has little to learn from a CP. The Opinionator knows what's what. The Answer Man, on the other hand, is desperately eager to please, or to impress, with his quickness and brilliance. It might seem like this individual has to be the smartest person in the room, but more often, what he or she needs is to be valued, to be indispensable. Some think having the answer and having it right now is the hallmark of a great leader. In the film *Patton*, didn't the legendary general seem to have all the answers immediately and bark them as orders? There's a reason we have a lot of action films, and not many films about making tough decisions. The former are much more fun to watch. But in business, broadcasting an answer prematurely is one very effective way of killing what could be and should be a productive opportunity to listen and gain information. Insufficient discussion can lead you to act on a half-baked and overly simplistic understanding of a situation.

The Answer Man can be exasperating, because he rarely has just one answer. He can't stop. If you point out flaws in his hasty solutions, he has ready revisions at hand. "Well, sure, but then we just have to . . ." He just keeps coming at you, driven by his need to save the day. His impatience is his undoing.

These archetypes of bad listeners generally prove ineffective precisely because they spend too much time talking. They are so busy sending out information that they don't allow themselves to be receptive. So do we conclude that the quiet, polite listener is the good listener? Not necessarily.

How many times have you had this experience? You talk with a boss or a colleague, arguing your points elegantly and articulately. You're convinced that you're having an impact because the other person nods wisely at all the right moments, and laughs when he's supposed to. Maybe he even finishes some of your sentences, not in a rude way, but in a way that shows he is engaged with your train of thought. And then, as soon as you walk out of the meeting, you have the uncomfortable sense that he hasn't really heard a word you were saying; or maybe he heard it all and just didn't care. This guy is a great actor, and he has just put on a great show. He's the **Pretender**. The Pretender isn't really interested in what you have to say. Maybe he's already made up his mind on the subject; maybe he's distracted by other matters; maybe he has to put on a show of listening for political reasons. Whatever the reason, we'd all be better off if he would drop the pretense. I once worked with a CEO who believed that it was a manager's duty to be as genuine as possible. Listening can't be faked, he told me once, you're either in it 100 percent or you're totally out of it.

The greatest Pretender I ever came across was the CEO of a many-tentacled health care corporation, a man I always think of as the Suit. This man was straight out of central casting: good-looking and polished, clever and charming. He had all the right moves. You'd swear he was hanging on every word you uttered, and you'd walk out of his office feeling like a million bucks, won over completely by his knowing, empathetic smile. It might take a while, but eventually you'd realize that he hadn't acted on anything you said, even though he had given every indication he was processing what you had to say and was in agreement. The Suit firmly believed that it was his job to make all the stakeholders within the company feel like they were being heard, that they were connected to, and well cared for by, the people at the top. If that was his only mission, he accomplished it very well, but I had to ask, at what price? He let people talk, but he didn't take in what they were saying. He didn't have access to the valuable information from previous conversations when it came time to make decisions or take action. The result was a lot of ill-informed choices. He was great at making people feel good in superficial ways, but he was not a very effective manager. Watching the Suit at work, I once again learned that there is an enormous difference between merely placating an organization, and actually raising it to greater performance.

You are likely a good listener at times. However, if you are honest with yourself you will recognize that many of these archetypes of bad listening apply to you at different times and in different situations. You might be a Grouch on certain subjects or at different moments in the business cycle, but act more like a benign Pretender in other circumstances. You need to be able to recognize the behavior of each of these types—in yourself, as well as in others—as the first step toward improving your own listening skills and raising the overall level of communication and decision making in your organization.

We can use this list of poor-listening archetypes in much the same way a doctor might run down a checklist of possible symptoms. It's really only the first step in getting to a diagnosis, but it's a critical first step. Without it, we cannot begin to move toward a cure. In the next chapters, I'll suggest some simple strategies for getting us closer to that cure.

((3))

Respect Your Conversation Partner

Indra Nooyi, the CEO of PepsiCo, recalls in an interview with *Fortune* that the best advice her father gave her about working with others was, "Assume positive intent." If you do, she said, "You will be amazed at how your whole approach to a person or problem becomes very different. You are trying to understand and listen because at your basic core you are saying, 'Maybe they are saying something to me that I'm not hearing.'" Indeed, most people you work with want to do their job well—and to help you do yours better, too. Generally speaking, it's safe to assume that you have chosen your conversation partner, or they have chosen you, because of that implicit covenant.

In helping people do their jobs better, I've learned in my career that people often already possess a lot of the knowledge they need to solve the problem challenging them, but may not be aware of it. They may not have made the necessary connection between an information set and the question on the table. So I always assume going into a conversation that my CP has many of the necessary tools to develop a good solution. My role may simply be to help draw out that information or put it in a new light. Certainly I can describe many instances where good listeners have been able to draw information out of me that I never knew I had, and have helped me to reach better solutions as a result—sometimes to problems that I didn't think I would be able to solve. It took me some time and a few missteps to learn that my role wasn't to suggest an immediate solution to problems—like the Answer Man—but to provide a path for my CPs to follow toward answers they might already have. If I'm talking to someone who's been selling jet engines for thirty years, I've got to respect that he knows what's going on in his industry, and somewhere within that knowledge lies the solution to a problem he wishes to discuss.

Here is a straightforward example of what I mean. I remember a meeting I had with a group of engineers at a large industrial company with a major R & D operation. I was there with the company's chief marketing officer (CMO), who was concerned about a new product introduction that had fallen flat. This company had traditionally been dominated by engineers who were usually excellent product developers. But they were puzzled by this particular product's failure to launch. As the CMO and I began speaking with the engineers about the new technology that went into the product, I remember being struck by their passion; these men and women were true inventors, and they conveyed their genuine excitement about the new device, which really did seem to be unique and ingenious. We had to keep stopping them to get them to explain various pieces of technical language. Eventually they were able to convey to us why it was revolutionary. They described how it was far more efficient than comparable products on the market and that it was easier to use, install, and maintain.

After a few minutes, the chief marketing officer, who had been listening intently, prompted them with a respectful leading question:

"But we haven't sold as many as you thought we would in the first three months, right?"

"Well, actually, we haven't sold any!" the leader of their team said. "We think this product is a game changer, we know how great it is. But it hasn't been selling. And we're not sure why."

After a pause to make sure the engineer had nothing more to add, the CMO said, "Well, you guys sure seem certain that this is a great product. And you've convinced the two of us pretty well. It seems that customers should be tripping over themselves to place their orders. So assuming it's not the product's quality that's off, what else are your customers telling you about the product?"

"We haven't spoken to any customers, so we're not sure," the engineer replied.

We both blanched. The CMO asked, "Why haven't you talked to the customers themselves?"

"Well, we developed this product under close wraps and we thought it would just speak for itself. But maybe not. Maybe we ought to push it a little more. I guess its good traits aren't so obvious if you don't know a lot about it."

The engineer had hit the nail on the head. There was nothing wrong with the device itself, but customers were wary about switching to something new and untested. They hadn't yet been convinced of the specs being touted by the sales team. As soon as these engineers got on the phone with their counterparts within the customers' organizations, they could explain the product's features just as convincingly as they had to us, this time without needing to dumb down the technical language! The game was on. Within weeks the company had received a batch of orders for the product, which ultimately ended up being exactly the kind of game changer that the engineers had predicted. The engineers had the answer to the problem all along. If the CMO and I had been looking at the problem alone, we might have suspected a shortcoming with the product itself. But, after some good listening and pointed questioning, the CMO extracted a much better solution from the engineers themselves. She didn't lecture them on good marketing techniques and didn't belittle their approach; she listened and asked the right questions in a respectful manner.

Of course, sometimes it is *you*, not your CP, who needs to provide the solution to a problem, and you engage your CP because you think he or she might be able to help. Here, again, the conversation depends on respect. Revelations and insights can come from unexpected places, so the best listeners solicit information from sources far and wide, knowing that any of their colleagues might have a surprising nugget of wisdom to offer. Managers often bucket their colleagues into certain roles and assume they can provide useful insight only into areas that are close to their expertise. They'll talk to their marketing associate about how to better promote products in Europe, but won't explore that person's views on operations or strategy. Respect means taking seriously everything people say to you, and giving them the benefit of the doubt. Even that quiet intern in the sales department might be able to offer a morsel of information that could help you arrive at a better solution.

I was lucky enough to have this lesson drilled into me at a relatively early stage of my career, not by a business professional, but a professor in medical school. George Engel developed a model of medicine that he dubbed "biopsychosocial," and it was essentially all about listening. He believed that a doctor could diagnose people far more accurately by using gentle questioning to tease out a deep and broad array of information—about their lives, their habits, their families, their jobs, anything that might (or might not) be relevant. "The patient is your teacher," he once said. "The clinical triad is observation, introspection, and dialogue . . . it's a negotiation." He also introduced us to the idea that each patient he treated was a study with an "N of one." What he meant by this was that each person was a case unto himself whose ailments and characteristics were so idiosyncratic as to be incomparable to those of anyone else. I have often thought this lesson applies quite well to good business listening. Each CP is unique, a person with his or her own set of experiences, opinions, viewpoints, ideas, and insights. And for that reason, each one is worthy of your time and attention.

The manager I encountered who demonstrated the most wonderful way of getting information, and showing respect for those who gave it to him, was the chief operating officer (COO) of a hospital. This man loved to walk. He covered the hallways of that hospital thousands of times, talking to everyone. He was an interesting fellow to behold. He was completely bald, and when he spoke to people he had a way of opening his eyes as wide as he could, like an owl peering at you from behind his thick-rimmed glasses. There was nothing of the Pretender about this man; this expression would naturally come across his face whether he was talking to the hospital's CFO, the custodian polishing the floors, or a patient's family. I discovered that these endless dialogues were motivated by much more than a desire to foster good morale. He remarked to me once that he simply couldn't run a place as complex as a hospital without soliciting information and ideas from everyone. He respected each and every employee and patient and they all returned that respect. During each exchange he would be sure to make a mental note of one idea or interesting tidbit that he could then use to start a conversation when they next met. This was a demonstration to each individual not only that he had been listening but that he had connected with their ideas and opinions. This COO succeeded because he was utterly democratic. He opened his mind to the possibility that everyone around him was smart in his or her own way and had a good idea or two. He approached every conversation with this attitude, and not just for his own benefit. Like the former New York City mayor Ed Koch, he was always asking, "How am I doing?" The difference was that he'd also ask, "How are you doing?" He meant both questions sincerely, and invited everyone to share with him a problem that he might help solve.

A great motivator, to be sure, but what made this COO a great manager was his ability to create concrete actions based on the input he received during his walkabouts. Whether it concerned signage in the hallways or how often examination rooms were cleaned, or even how staff greeted incoming patients, he made sure to mine every conversation for those pearls of insight.

Of course, some conversations are not explicitly about problem solving. You might be debriefing after an intense negotiation, or giving feedback on a presentation, or even just checking in on the health of your colleague's mother. However, respect and good listening are still important. As the COO of the hospital demonstrated to me, even trivial pieces of information or seemingly unrelated ideas can be helpful later in solving problems. This man wouldn't extract some blinding new insight from every conversation he had with the custodian; but every once in a while that custodian would say something that caused the COO to rethink a problem or situation. How many times have we heard political pundits comment that U.S. presidents operate in a bubble, with limited exposure to the everyday plights and difficulties of living in America? How is the president supposed to govern, they argue, when he doesn't understand what the effects of his decisions will be? In fairness to the president, it is often very difficult to break out of this bubble. Not so, though, for managers of corporations. Breaking out of your bubble and sourcing ideas and information from those at every level of your organization—as well as the customers, suppliers, and competitors outside it—is the only way to have a rich understanding of the business problems you'll face.

Even if you don't get to any revelations, a comment or idea may prove useful somewhere down the road.

Respecting your colleagues can also pay off over time, by making them more willing to share with you their ideas the next time around. Conversations don't have to be immediately productive to be useful or important; sometimes their value lies in how they seed better communication in the future. Take, for example, those conversations that are very short or directive. These are the ones my clients like to cite when I explain this idea of universal respect. They'll say: "That's all fine and well, but my day only has so many hours in it. And sometimes I have no choice but to tell people what I need them to do or ask them quickly for something I want done." Fair enough. Not all conversations are about problem solving, and many high-level managers have directive styles and a get-it-done attitude. Yet respect is important, even in these instances. Demonstrating respect as you're passing on an instruction or request lays the foundation for fruitful communication later on down the road. If your team members know you respect them, and can sense it even in your commands, they will be more willing to offer their genuine thoughts during that next problem-solving conversation.

Kevin Sharer, the Amgen CEO, is a fine example of an executive who has worked out how to balance this tone of respect with the need to move forward and get to better decisions and actions. He will be the first to tell you how important mutual respect is in his organization. In fact, he often will follow up on a conversation with a personalized note that reiterates some of the main points that he heard. This not only shows his CP that he was listening but it also serves the useful purpose of ensuring that there is absolute clarity in the understanding of the ideas. But he also recognizes that respect for your colleagues must be coupled with another kind of respect—for the fast-paced nature of the business environment. So when he has a conversation, he signals to his CP that the sole purpose is to get to a better answer. I've observed other good listeners demonstrate an approach similar to Sharer's. At the same time that they probe for more information, they will search for what could be called a "trial close." "So are you telling me I should do this?" they will ask. "Does this mean you think we move in this direction?" Their tone won't be sharp; rather it is directed and focused. They invite creativity and new ideas, as long as their CPs can demonstrate that the thought connects somehow with the question they are trying to answer or the decision they are trying to make. By forcing their CPs to focus their thinking in this way, they can add a tremendous amount of value to the creative ideas they espouse.

I've now explained the importance of respecting the intellectual potential of everyone with whom you work. But respect also entails making allowances for individuals' foibles and distinct peculiarities. Not everyone is going to adapt to you, so the best listeners learn how to adapt to others. In this sense, the best listeners are chameleons. They recognize early on the particular paces and cadences of their CP, and adapt their listening accordingly. In fact, some listeners will understand that a change in their CP's style signals a shift in mindset, which in turn can guide the listener to adjust his questioning.

Let's go back to my friend the hospital manager. I already described him to you as being like an owl, but in another way he was much like a chameleon. He had the remarkable ability to change his listening style to match the styles of those around him. Because this was such a large hospital, there were people from all walks of life who worked there. Some were from the Deep South, others were blue-blooded northeasterners. Some were old and others were young. Some had not graduated from high school, while others had advanced medical degrees. And of course, as in any large organization, there was a fair share of quirky oddballs and eccentric misfits. This man could talk to all of them. If they spoke slowly, he too would slow his pace (he used to remind me that slow talking did not necessarily mean slow thinking). If they jumped around a lot from subject to subject, he would jump along with them.

He also had a knack for recognizing when a pace change was not a question of style, but a reflection of his CP's thought process. I remember watching him in conversation with a nurse-manager. She kept doubling back and repeating herself. Normally she was a pretty articulate person, but on this occasion he realized there was something unusual going on. At a pause in her speech, he surprised me by asking gently, "You don't quite agree with me on this one, do you? Why is that?" She sighed in relief and explained what it was that had actually been bugging her.

This COO had developed a sixth sense. He could pick up when and where a change in style meant that something wasn't right. I call it a sixth sense, because it can be very difficult to develop. Sometimes a style shift can indicate a lack of resolution, sometimes a lack of agreement, and sometimes it really is just style. Practice helps, of course, and with time good managers learn how to feel out these situations. In the meantime, my advice is to ask probing questions when you sense that your CP's style is confusing you. Something like: "Am I missing something here?" Or: "Are we on the same page with this?" At least that gives your CPs the permission to explain themselves fully.

A shift in your CP's pace or style of speaking is just one of many possible nonverbal cues that you will pick up as you improve your listening skills. Nonverbal communication is a field of social psychology that has produced a wealth of literature. I'm therefore not going to spend a great deal of time discussing the possible meanings of all the nonverbal cues you will encounter in your business conversations. What's more important than having a road map for what each nonverbal sign might mean is to develop listening habits that allow you to be on the lookout for nonverbal behavior. That's part of the reason why it's so important to keep quiet. If it's true, as psychologists claim, that a remarkable amount of social meaning is communicated through nonverbal behavior, then you'll be missing out on a lot of information while you spout windy sentiments or lengthy explanations.

Of course, you are not going to derive useful information from every single nod or change in intonation. But in certain cases, non-verbal communication can be invaluable. For example, if you feel like there is a lack of alignment between the verbal messages being con-veyed and the nonverbal messages being given off, that should prob-ably set off some alarm bells in your head about the quality of the information you're hearing. However, I don't want to make you believe that paying attention to nonverbal behavior is all about catch-ing your CPs in lies or obfuscations. Ultimately, it's still about respect. Part of respecting the CP while you listen is remaining attuned to the verbal *and* nonverbal messages being conveyed and understanding that both may contain useful and important information for your business.

Now that I have made the case for respecting each and every CP you encounter, I have to admit that occasionally you're sure to meet some people whose conversational style is such that it can, by itself, prevent effective communication. The world is full of all kinds of infuriating folks—jokers and kibitzers, narcissists and bullies, ram-blers and pontificators—all of whom can drain the energy from a room and derail a conversation even before it gets going. There will be times when these people will be too much for you to bear. Your patience will run out, and your blood will boil. Try as you might, you won't be able to get past your own annoyance or frustration to access the tools of good listening, no matter how skilled or practiced you are. It's natural at times to feel this way, as long as you are able to step back just far enough to recognize your response and deal with it. You can try to salvage the conversation with subtle cues: "I'd love to trade stories about this later, as soon as we make some progress on this question." Or, you might address the situation more directly, if you judge that your CP would be receptive: "You know, this isn't quite working for me. I hear what you're saying, but right now, I need to limit the discussion to the specific agenda points."

If these gambits don't bring your CP closer to your wavelength, and the conversation continues to frustrate you, you can always recommend a postponement of the discussion, perhaps suggesting that more information is required. You could even suggest a set of specific discussion questions, almost as homework, if for no other reason than to give more shape and focus to the next attempt. If you feel that the prospects for a future face-to-face conversation are equally bleak and if the circumstances allow, you can simply transform the discussion into written form: "Maybe it would speed things along if you could put your thoughts and suggestions into a short memo for me to read?"

Clearly, conversations like these will not be very productive. Indeed, you may find that, despite all your good intentions, several of your conversations in a given day aren't very productive. Sometimes people don't have the answers to their own questions, or can't give you much new insight into the problem you're trying to solve, or are just downright obnoxious and bombastic. The point is to approach each conversation from the outset assuming that you *might* be able to learn something new. And if you find that you can't, don't let that taint the next conversation you have with the same individual. Even if you're completely skeptical about what your CP is saying, you can keep the channels of communication open, and maintain that covenant of respect, by acknowledging them without agreeing: "I hear you, but I'm just not prepared to agree yet. Maybe I could hear a little more at a later date?"

Sometimes I have found that it works to state outright that I have respect for my CP. It can be quite a powerful way to open a conversation. Though it sounds trite, if said in good faith and communicated earnestly it can be a remarkably effective way to put your CP at ease and encourage him or her to offer up fresher and braver ideas. It's a way of making your conversation covenant explicit, and it can provide a solid foundation for good listening and powerful problem solving. Try it sometime. Start off a conversation with a colleague you trust by saying: "You know, talking to you always helps my thinking." See what happens!

How to Keep Quiet—
Most of the Time

Chances are that you've heard someone invoking the "80/20 rule" somewhere recently. Maybe it had to do with the distribution of wealth or resources, or maybe it was a reference to the productivity of your workforce, but the 80/20 rule has become regnant in a wide variety of disciplines. It applies to listening as well. My guideline is that my conversation partner should be speaking 80 percent of the time, while I speak only 20 percent of the time. Further, I seek to maximize my 20 percent. I can make my speaking time count by spending as much of it as possible posing questions, rather than holding forth with my opinions and observations.

Once, after I explained this formula in a university lecture, an MBA student cleverly challenged my 80/20 rule with a question: "What happens if you have two good listeners?"

My answer: "In that case, congratulations! You folks will have productive—and very short—conversations!"

It sounds easy enough—just keep your mouth shut, right?—but it's much easier said than done. This is why I've devoted an entire chapter to something that seems so simple and straightforward. Most of us are naturally inclined to speak our minds. Forcing yourself to control that impulse is about as easy as trying not to flinch at the sound of a startling noise. Still, with patience and practice, you can learn to control your urge to speak, and improve the quality and effectiveness of your conversations.

I understand that people in leadership positions feel a certain pressure to steer or direct or control conversations within their organizations, but don't be misled: Your choosing to listen more than speak does not mean you've ceded control of a conversation. Well-directed questioning and minimal but well-timed commentary can help people bring forward new facts, open their minds, think in new ways, and come up with better ideas. A good listener can use savvy Socratic questioning to move any conversation in a specific desired direction, not necessarily to produce a predetermined outcome, but to cover essential ground—and these techniques can also help unearth buried information you weren't expecting to find. Ultimately, a good listener gains more control over the problem at hand and comes to better decisions.

Learning to keep your mouth shut can have other, less tangible benefits as well. Those of you who have visited New York City restaurants will know that tables are often pushed tightly together, so that you are sitting cheek-by-jowl with the party next to yours, virtually bumping elbows with them as you inevitably hear most of their conversation. For some reason, I often get seated at these restaurants next to a man and a woman who are obviously on their first date. I am always struck by how frequently the eyes of one member of these would-be couples slowly glaze over while the other rambles on about his or her exploits and accomplishments. Sure, rambling is a natural response to an awkward social situation. I always say to myself that if only this chatty person would stop trying to impress a date, who's probably already predisposed to be impressed, and start trying to draw him or her out a little, the two of them might decide they've hit the jackpot, instead of quickly writing off that first date as their last.

It's a simple life lesson that translates almost directly to management. I've heard from CEOs who believe that their reputation as a good listener has made them more sympathetic, even more attractive, to their staffs. Of course, listening is a necessary tool, not merely a matter of personal style. The point is not to be a more popular manager, but that workers are more likely to be forthcoming with new ideas when they are confident that someone is listening to them. Leaders don't need to act on, or even agree with, every new idea that circulates through an organization; what's important is that each idea is attended to seriously and respectfully. That alone establishes a comfort level that will facilitate the free flow of information and ideas.

John Bryan, who served for twenty-five years as the Chairman and CEO of Sara Lee Corporation, believes that a manager is not free to choose whether to get information out of people within his organization; it is his responsibility. He would say it defines the job. He understands the value of remaining receptive and creating an atmosphere of openness. "If you're a manager who doesn't want to hear other options," says Bryan, "you won't hear them."

Management consultants, like many business leaders, enjoy talking, and I'm no exception. In part, that's what we get paid to do. When we impress our clients with flashes of insight, we feel like we're earning our keep. But, early in my career, I had an experience that made me realize I was focusing on the wrong half of the conversation. I had traveled to the offices of an important client, whom I was eager to impress. I remember entering the room and finding him seated somewhat regally at his conference table with his number-two man at his side. My no-nonsense client, a granite block of a man from the American heartland, scrutinized me over the top of his reading glasses.

He laid out the problem at hand: "The budget for next year just doesn't work, and we are asking our employees to make some tough changes."

All I heard was his concern about the budget, and without missing a beat, I responded, "There are several ways to address your cost problem . . ." I immediately began reeling off what I thought were some excellent suggestions for streamlining his business. My speech gained momentum as I barreled ahead with my ideas. My client listened silently, and attentively, or so it seemed. He didn't say a word, or even move, except to cock his head from time to time. When he finally lifted a hand off the table to reach for a pen, I kept up my oration, but watched with some annoyance as he wrote on a small notepad, tore off the sheet of paper and handed it to his associate. I saw a smile flit almost imperceptibly across that man's face as he read the note.

I was already a bit peeved that the client had displayed no reaction to my brilliant ideas, but this little note, passed as though between two schoolboys, was just too much. I stopped talking and asked what was written on the paper.

My client nodded to his associate. "Show him."

The man leaned across the table and handed me the note. My client had scribbled only eight words: "What the hell is this guy talking about?"

Fortunately, I was able to step back and see the humor in the situation, or I might have ended my consulting career right then and there. I had been a fool. My ego had gotten in the way of my exercising any good listening habits. But I was able to look at the incident as a learning opportunity, and fortunately, the lesson was relatively obvious. I had failed to listen. If I had paid closer attention to the way in which my client had outlined his problem, if I had probed more deeply with a few follow-up questions before launching into my little speech, I would have understood that his real concern was finding ways to keep his staff motivated while the company was shrinking. And then, after I failed to listen, I compounded the error by failing to keep quiet. Luckily for me, on this occasion I was able to get a second date.

Think about the Opinionator, the Preambler, or the Answer Man from chapter 2. These archetypal bad listeners all make the same basic mistake—they don't keep quiet. It's not simply that they talk when they should be listening; it's that their input doesn't serve the conversation. It doesn't focus or elaborate or illuminate the CP's thoughts. Rather, it just serves to somehow reinforce the listener's status, burnish his or her self-image, or provide a bunch of irrelevant ideas. The problem, as I have already mentioned, is that showmanship is so often associated with great leadership in business, even though a number of business professors have suggested that extroversion and flamboyance are poor indicators of success in business. Indeed, one study by Ulrike Malmendier and Geoffrey Tate, called "Superstar CEOs," finds that managers become *less* effective the more famous and notable they become. In another study, called "Which CEO Characteristics and Abilities Matter?" Steven Kaplan, Mark Klebanov, and Morten Sorensen argue that qualities like persistence, analytical thoroughness, efficiency, humility, and diligence are shown to correlate the most with success. I have found that many executives with these critical business traits manifest them in the way they listen. They keep quiet, to begin with, and then they use thoughtful, persistent, and diligent listening to get the information they need and solve the problems before them.

At this point you may suspect that there's something of a mixed message in my admonition to keep quiet on the one hand and to make yourself a proactive, probing listener on the other. The fact is that to be a good listener, you must walk a very fine line between keeping quiet and participating in such a way as to advance the conversation. How do you know when to jump in? I like to ask myself a simple question: Will my comment or question cause my CP to say *more*? I don't just mean more words. I mean more analysis, more information, and more insights. It's a useful test: if my input can cause my CP to go deeper, provide more detail, flesh out more options or in any way enhance his or her train of thought, it's worth my jumping in. It might even be my duty to jump in. However, if my input will inhibit or derail or corrupt my CP's ideas, or worse yet only show off my own ideas, it's my duty to keep it to myself, at least for that moment.

There are some people with a natural intuitive grasp of where that line falls between input and interruption, but the rest of us have to work at it. John McLaughlin, the former CIA number two, is someone who seems to do this effortlessly. But when I asked him about it, he said that he thinks very consciously about when to keep quiet and when to interrupt. It's a skill that he has had to hone. His advice is to be as neutral and emotionless as possible when listening, always delaying the rebuttal and withholding the interruption. Still, he acknowledges that interrupting with a question can be necessary, at times to speed up the communication process, and at other times to redirect it. He advises managers not to be in a hurry, though—if a matter gets to your level, he says, it is probably worth your spending some time on it.

Sometimes management teams develop their own unique listening dynamics that only they can follow. I'm sure you know lifelong friends who finish each other's thoughts and step on each other's sentences. Or perhaps you've somehow gotten too close to a gaggle of teenagers and tried to follow their conversation, in which one teen's speech flows out of the middle of another's, and then gives way to the next. It might sound like machine-gun fire to the uninitiated, but the kids in the group always seem to know what's going on. And then, of course, there's the classic scene, caricatured in movies like *My Big Fat*

Greek Wedding of the boisterous and chaotic family dinner with every-body talking at the same time—or yelling, as often as not. Nobody seems to be listening.

None of the listening going on in these three scenarios is optimal, but that's not to say there's no communication going on. In each case, custom and shared experience combine to allow for a level of familiarity that exists only in a handful of organizations. Relationships of long standing often allow for a special kind of shorthand communication. There's a priceless moment in the film *Broadcast News* when Albert Brooks says to Holly Hunter, "Meet me at the place by the thing where we went that time," and she knows exactly what he's talking about. Occasionally, I've met executives who have worked together for many years who can communicate in this way. I've sat with managers of long tenure whose staffs understand the message in every nod of the head or flick of the hand. But as companies change hands with staggering frequency, and management teams swoop in and out like commandos, this kind of relationship feels more and more like a relic of a bygone era.

Figuring out when to interrupt has become even harder as rules of behavior have relaxed and the pace of exchanges has quickened. In business and academia and government, we now place a higher value on informality, which, for better or worse, has engendered what I sometimes feel is a culture of interruption. We also respect people who are sharp with their insights or quick on their feet. Think about episodes from the TV series *The West Wing*. Those presidential staffers are always interrupting and finishing each other's sentences, admittedly with a pretty lucid and crisp comment. Even young staffers quip jovially with their superiors, and the back-and-forth is continuous to the point of being grueling. But this is drama. In real-time business situations, a sharp tongue or a quick retort can be a hindrance to solving problems.

Often, in business or organizational settings, our tendency to interrupt people in conversation arises from our impatience to seek closure, or our need to stroke our egos in conversation. As if those natural human foibles weren't enough to contend with, the proliferation of new information technology has, in some ways, exacerbated the problem. Every individual has access to an inexhaustible deluge of information, as well as instantaneous communications, at their fingertips. Whether it's e-mail or cell-phone calls or instant messaging or postings on our virtual walls, we've become inured to listening to multiple voices and to constantly diverting our focus and attention. Not surprisingly, the mind-set created by these devices is seeping into face-to-face conversation, especially in the generation just now entering the work force.

The first thing to do when you feel the urge to interrupt is to—keep quiet! You need to control your instincts and reflexes when you're listening. Don't say anything—no responses, no comments—before taking a moment to think about how it will affect the speaker and the course of the conversation. As a practical matter, when I consciously pause in a conversation, I like to count five beats in my head. Now, if you succeed in keeping still and quiet, you might create a moment or two of uncomfortable silence. Don't be afraid of that. Most people abhor silence, just as nature abhors a vacuum, and they have a natural tendency to fill empty silences with commentary. However, you could be very surprised by what insightful comments your CPs blurt out during these lulls. Sometimes I find it helps to simply nod a little, just so they know I'm not zoning out. Otherwise, I wait and listen for what else they have to say.

Also, don't anticipate the period at the end of the sentence, the way the crowd at a ball game starts cheering in the last three measures of the national anthem. There are still some people left out there who think and speak in paragraphs, and might have more to say. So if a CP is done speaking and seems to be inviting me to respond, I consciously pause and wait to see if he or she will keep talking. Further, if you sense the CP has more to say, but is holding back for some reason, say something that will draw them out, and encourage them to complete the thought. You never know when the next thing they say will be the key to unlocking a problem. I like the simple statement, "Tell me more about that." Try to sound inviting, rather than prosecutorial; you're giving them permission to rephrase or to expand on an idea. It's extraordinary how effective a simple question like that can be.

Sometimes it is necessary to break the silence. After all, I did suggest that you should be speaking 20 percent of the time. How do you know when to open your mouth? When is it appropriate to interrupt? A basic rule I like to impose on myself is to phrase any interruptions or responses I make as questions. If I disagree with a statement, I'll package my disagreement in a probing question. If I want to break down an issue further, I'll ask my CP if he or she has thought about it in such-and-such a way. If I don't like the path the conversation is taking, I'll redirect it with a question.

To help make sure I jump in only when appropriate, I keep a short list of questions in my mind that helps discipline me in my interruptions. I try to limit my interjections to moments when I can guide the conversation into areas that will be more useful for me and my CP. I ask myself:

1. Do I need any clarification?

2. Do I want to hear more about this issue, or one that has come before?

3. Do I need to parse an issue to focus on a certain aspect?

4. Do I want to head down a different line of discussion?

5. Is there a counterargument or new perspective I want to pose that might cause my CP to reexamine his point of view?

6. Do I need to end the conversation?

If I can answer yes to any one of these questions, then, and only then, do I feel comfortable jumping into the conversation and putting in my two cents.

The 20 percent of your time spent talking should mostly be filled with questions seeking to steer the conversation into more productive terrain. The 80/20 rule should lead to shorter and more focused conversations. Your CP will do most of the talking, but with your focused questioning and well-timed interruptions he will be able to *convey more*. You should think of your role in all this as akin to that of the rudder on the ship—steering, guiding, and adjusting. Occasionally you will prod or dig for more. The key is to discipline yourself and your CP into generating better ideas and more information faster and more efficiently.

Anyone at any level in an organization benefits from polishing these communication skills, but the advantages to a manager are powerful:

▶ There are few things as attractive in a manager as a reputation for being "easy to talk to." It's a character trait that invites openness and honesty, and generates both information and ideas.

▶ If you learn to listen with the right kind of engagement— asking the right questions at the right time—you'll make people think about their own ideas with more depth, breadth, and clarity.

▶ You'll sift through the overload of information in conversation and get to the important issues more quickly and more consistently.

▶ You'll move more efficiently from deliberation to decision, and from decision to action.

How might these principles play themselves out in the real world? Let's return to that fateful meeting in which I nearly ended my consulting career. When the client explained his problem, that the only way to make his budget work was to demand more from his employees, I failed to take any time to process his statement, or to allow him to elaborate. I heard only the invitation for me to parade my knowledge. What could I have done differently?

To begin with, I could have simply taken a breath. If I had waited a few beats, chances are that the client would have filled the silence, elaborating on his statement in ways that would have shed more light on the issue.

Let's assume I paused, and he went on. "Costs are always a concern. But it's the employee piece that's really eating at me. I'm worried about what my employees will think if I start cutting costs left and right."

Here again, it might have been best just to wait. Though with this he may seem to be looking for a response, I might get a bit more valuable information out of him by letting him fill that moment of silence. Maybe I nod a little, just to let him know I'm considering what he's saying.

Perhaps he would go on: "Honestly, it's not the line workers that

I'm most worried about; they're pretty resilient and they get that we're facing tough times. It's the guys closer to the top who concern me. They think that these budget cuts are counter to a strategy that they're committed to. I'm worried about an exodus if we start cutting back."

Now, without saying a word, my CP has taken me to the crux of where his problem lies. If he didn't fill the silence with this response, perhaps I could have elicited it by asking: "Can you say a little more about that?"

As he goes through this explanation I would be running through my head all those questions I listed earlier to see if I need to jump in at any time. Maybe I want to understand more about the old strategy: "What is this strategy they're so committed to? And how do they understand the new strategy?"

Or maybe I need to better understand which employees are at risk: "Are you worried about certain employees in particular?"

Or, alternatively, maybe I think he's being too quick to dismiss the possibility that the front-line workers won't balk at the prospect of cuts or layoffs: "What makes you so confident that your line workers won't be just as upset about the cuts? Have you thought about whether the union might play a role?"

Depending on which question I deem to be most important and the order in which I ask them, the conversation might travel down several different roads. At each crossroad, I would be sure to repeat my process: pausing, resisting my impulse to jump in, probing with questions when appropriate, and steering us toward a better solution. Remember that in chapter 3 I said that most managers have the answer to their own questions? If I had followed these steps, I might have discovered that this man had everything he needed to get him to a workable solution, and that my role was simply to prod and guide.

In his poem "If," Rudyard Kipling advises the following: "And yet don't look too good, nor talk too wise." It's sound advice, both for management and for life. Indeed, it is an important step toward learning how to be a better listener: Don't posture or pose, don't pontificate or bluster, don't be the Preambler or the Opinionator or the Answer Man. Rather, stop, pause, think, and then, if necessary, ask a question. These are techniques designed to get us to that ideal 80/20 listening equilibrium.

Challenge All Assumptions

The summer before I went off to college, my best friend landed the job of clubhouse manager for the Rochester Red Wings, who were, at the time, the Baltimore Orioles' farm team in my hometown. I got to hang out with him at the ball park, where I had the unique opportunity to observe the team's manager for that summer, the legendary Earl Weaver, who went on to lead the Orioles to four American League pennants and a World Series title. Sportscasters of the time referred to Weaver with such epithets as "fiery" or "cantankerous," but they considered him to be a baseball genius. To my eighteen-year-old eyes, he was nothing short of terrifying—the meanest and most profane man I'd ever met.

Weaver wasn't really a listener; he was more a screamer in a perpetual state of rage. When a young player would make a really boneheaded play—a mental error—Weaver would take him aside and ask for an explanation. "Why did you throw to second base when the runner was on his way to third?" He'd wait to hear every detail of the player's reasoning, for the sole purpose of savagely tearing it apart, usually in the foulest language imaginable and at the top of his lungs.

But every now and then, the great Earl Weaver would be brought up short. He'd hear something in the player's explanation that would make him stop and reconsider. "But I've seen that guy take a big wide turn several times, but then come back to the bag. I thought maybe if I got the ball to second really fast, we could catch him." Weaver knew just about everything there was to know about base-ball, and on the basis of that accumulated wisdom, throwing to sec-ond base was just wrong. As ornery as he was, however, I suspect that Earl Weaver had the innate ability to absorb the new, relevant infor-mation that upended his standard working assumptions. And, in doing so, the vociferous Weaver became a listener.

When Earl Weaver published his autobiography, he called it *It's What You Learn after You Know It All That Counts*. Who can say whether this Zen-like philosophy was really in keeping with the Weaver every-body knew, but that title has stuck with me for years. The ornery Weaver had found a perfect way to state one of the cornerstone prin-ciples of listening: to get what we need from our conversations, we must be prepared to challenge long-held and cherished assumptions. Nobody makes good decisions sitting alone in an office. I'm not refer-ring to the countless minor judgment calls a businessperson makes every day, but about the more major calls or, alternatively, about a series of decisions that appear routine but that add up to something much bigger. One brain alone can rarely solve big problems.

I like to go into a conversation asking, "What do we both need to get from this interaction so that we can come out smarter? What do we know or think we know and, of what remains, how much can we find out and how much can't we?" The latter is just as critical as the former because it highlights where you'll be basing your decisions on imperfect or incomplete information. To get the knowable facts, you usually have to engage many people, and you may have to talk to even more folks to determine what is *not* knowable. But many businesspeople struggle because they are carrying around bad facts or bad ideas. The reason is that they never think to relax their assumptions and open themselves up to other possibilities that can be drawn from conversations with others. Assumptions are the biggest barriers most people face in getting the crucial facts and ideas that lead to good judgment. They think they know it all—or at least know what's most important—and stop listening to anything that might undermine these beliefs. Indeed, when it comes to assumptions, Earl really did have it right: It's what you learn *after* you know it all that counts.

Much of the time, we remain blissfully ignorant of the assumptions that govern our decision making. In many cases, we don't become fully conscious of them until they are challenged. And then, our natural stubbornness kicks in, and we often dig our heels in, certain of the correctness of those operating assumptions. The problem is that unfortunately, this feeling of certainty does not guarantee that something is actually true. It's not necessarily the end product of infallible reasoning. Rather, certainty is a feeling, a good feeling—like calm or even joy. The neurologist Robert Burton tackles this phenomenon of feeling like you know something in his eye-opening book entitled *On Being Certain: Believing You Are Right Even When You're Not.* Burton challenges our acceptance of fundamental concepts like reason and objectivity, which he describes as the "twin pillars of certainty." Burton assembles a wealth of experimental evidence to argue that the feeling of certainty is just that—a feeling, or mental state resulting from chemical reactions in the brain—and doesn't necessarily connect to actual facts. We can feel certain that interest rates will remain low, that our competitor will not introduce the new product until next spring, or that the new market will grow at least three times as fast as the more mature markets. If these "certainties" prove to be false assumptions, they can be truly toxic to your business. Conversations provide occasions to examine and challenge our assumptions. Certainty, and the assumptions it guards, wreak havoc because they shut down our hearing. The refrain, "I know the answer already" is a sure symptom of all the pathologies exhibited by the Opinionator, the Preambler, the Answer Man, and the other archetypal bad listeners I've described.

In his book *Why the West Rules—for Now*, the historian and archaeologist Ian Morris reminds us that humankind's ability to predict how the future will unfold has been marked by many failures. The trajectory of history has been consistent only in its ability to confuse and surprise those who were sure they knew how it would evolve. Morris cites the Nobel Prize–winning chemist Richard Smalley, who used to poke fun at the certainty that his scientific colleagues often evinced. "When a scientist says something is possible," he would say, "they're probably underestimating how long it will take. But if they say it's impossible, they're probably wrong."

Yet we all fall into the same trap over and over again: we let our assumptions and preconceptions color every dialogue and every introduction of a new idea, and often, those assumptions keep a good idea or a unique insight from ever seeing the light of day. This is partly because it's difficult, and often exhausting, to maintain an awareness of ingrained beliefs and to constantly be on the lookout for evidence that challenges them. John McLaughlin, of the CIA, told me that to overcome this tendency toward cognitive inertia he had a sign hanging in his office proclaiming: SUBVERT THE DOMINANT PARADIGM!

One of the true masters of testing and challenging assumptions is the great fictional detective Sherlock Holmes. Holmes's style of deductive reasoning is one of his defining traits—we all remember him chastising his colleague Watson for failing to reach conclusions that Holmes considers to be "quite elementary." In fact, on most occasions, what Holmes has deduced is not elementary, but quite astonishing. His remarkable ability is built on an understanding that assumptions should never be fixed, but rather must be constantly questioned and revised. At one point in the Arthur Conan Doyle novel *The Hound of the Baskervilles,* Holmes sharply interrupts Watson, who is barreling ahead with a line of reasoning: "A great mystery to me," Watson says, "is why this hound, presuming that all our conjectures are correct—" But Holmes cuts him off: "I presume nothing." It is a simple statement, but perhaps gets to the essence of what makes Holmes such a brilliant problem solver. He develops well-reasoned hypotheses based on whatever evidence he has, but never accepts these hypotheses as fact. He presumes nothing and therefore never rules out other possibilities. In another instance, from *The Sign of Four,* Holmes once again chastises Watson for failing to be more deliberate in his reasoning: "How often have I said to you that when you have eliminated the impossible, whatever remains, however improbable, must be the truth?" Unless it is truly impossible, it cannot be entirely ruled out. This precept worked extraordinarily well for the fictional Holmes, and it can have powerful implications for us in business as well.

The truly good listeners, like Sherlock Holmes, never lose their ability to be surprised. I like to remind myself of the apocryphal story about the venerable physicist who has internalized a set of basic assumptions concerning the laws of gravity and inertia and simple Newtonian mechanics, but who also remains open to a universe of possibility. "If I throw a brick out of a window, and it goes *up,* you better believe I'm going to pay attention!"

It's easy to quip about always expecting the unexpected, but a really great listener takes this a couple of steps further. He embraces the unexpected, even actively seeks it out, which is, of course, much easier said than done. The U.S. Secretary of State traditionally keeps a counselor on staff, one of whose primary functions is to directly challenge his or her assumptions, so that the secretary has to consciously reevaluate his or her positions, either to make sure they hold up, or to discover their hidden flaws. Imagine: someone whose job it is to regularly go behind closed doors with one of the most important members of the national brain trust and say, in essence, "Are you sure about that?" What an amazing idea! Eliot Cohen, who served in this role under Secretary Condoleezza Rice, said that he would have many debates with the secretary about the issues she faced. She needed someone to spar with intellectually, to question her perspectives and to propose new possibilities.

There aren't too many companies or organizations that can afford to keep such a person on staff, but good leaders understand that, one way or another, they need to build this vital function into their institutional thinking. Daniel Vasella, the Chairman of the Swiss pharmaceutical company Novartis, is a great example of an executive who has figured this out. He believes that managers usually fail to listen because they have a hard time tolerating the unknown. Good listeners, he told me, have confidence that all the unknowns floating around in a good conversation will eventually be nailed down and better understood. These great listeners are comfortable with ambiguity, and thrive under the extra energy that it brings to their thinking. He describes the interactions he has with his people as the fuel to his problem solving, the occasions on which he generates new insights and hears new ideas. Listening is what revs him up; he needs it to propel his thinking and make the right decisions.

Vasella, like many other great listeners, has also trained himself to listen to what's not being said. The fact is that we most likely aren't even conscious of the assumptions that underlie every conversation.

No matter how good our intentions, or how hard we try, we cannot fully control the assumptions that take hold of our thinking. A generation of research and scholarship has brought to light the many ways in which our reason and intellect are less reliable than we often believe. For example, think for a moment of one particular psychological tendency referred to as the *status quo bias*, which describes the human inclination to unconsciously resist change. The subconscious finds safety and comfort in keeping things the way they are, even if things aren't so great. Change, on the other hand, even when our rational mind recognizes it as change for the better, causes anxiety. The status quo bias is commonly illustrated by the fact that in the U.S., only about a quarter of the population checks the organ-donor box on their driver's license, whereas in countries that ask you to check a box only if you *don't* want to become an organ donor, the same percentage of the population opts out of the volunteer program.

Now let's imagine how this kind of behavioral inertia can infect your listening. If you bring a set of fixed beliefs to a conversation, you've established a hurdle that your CP has to overcome just to get communications started. Changing your mind requires effort and conscious action—like making the decision to check off the organ-donor box—that humans naturally resist.

Several other biases have been shown to corrupt rationality. For instance, there's the *herding instinct*, which makes people want to conform to the behaviors or perceptions of the people around them, and which is often compounded by their tendency to assume a *false consensus* or overestimate the extent to which others share their perceptions or experiences. Planning is often complicated by our subconscious tendency toward *overconfidence* and our general inability to accurately estimate the pleasure or pain generated by a dramatic change of circumstance, which psychologists refer to as an *hedonic adaptation*.

I find it a fascinating and instructive exercise to look back at the

2008 financial crisis through this lens of the unconscious workings of the brain. Respected financial professionals appear to have been simply blinded by their assumptions. They felt certain they knew what they "knew." They allowed their decision making to be governed by any number of subconscious tendencies, from overconfidence to the status quo bias. Why else would banks feel so free to make those real-estate loans, or to buy up the mortgage-related debt of other institutions as a promising investment? The housing market had been rising for decades, and there seemed to be no safer investment available than the purchase of a new home. It had become part of the national ethos, and even when a few lonely voices occasionally sounded an alarm, no one heard. Obviously, the roots of the crisis are far more complex than the bursting housing bubble, but undeniably, the inability to reconsider this one set of assumptions nearly brought down an entire economy.

One wonders how good decisions ever get made, or how anyone could exercise good judgment, in the face of so many inborn obstacles, but of course it often occurs. And, you can increase the chances of getting to those good decisions if you listen in order to challenge what is taken as fact. It's important to remember that when it comes to challenging assumptions, I'm not necessarily talking about the big, obvious game changers that come up in business—the arrival of new technology, or the sudden opening or shutting down of international markets—but more often about subtle, even mundane matters, that can have far-reaching or profound ramifications. We don't spend much time thinking about whether a long-term supplier will always be there, whether the dollar will always be strong, or whether political stability in a major market will continue. And to get at those dusty assumptions under which we operate every day, we have to consciously, routinely question and challenge our thinking by listening to those who could have different facts or different perspectives.

The great listeners I've observed in business over the years are the ones who force themselves and their colleagues to identify and challenge assumptions as part of every strategic conversation. It's the only way they can squeeze every last drop of information or interpretation out of every discussion. They might ask their CP, "What are the three or four factors that make you think that?" Or the questions could be less specific, and designed simply to get the person to step back and listen to themselves and see if there's anything they want to rethink: "Are you saying that . . . ?" "Can you explain why that is?" These same listeners are also running their own assumptions through a similar diagnosis. They are always laying bare their assumptions for scrutiny.

Arne Duncan, the U.S. Secretary of Education, is one such listener. He believes that his listening improves when he has strong, tough people around him who will challenge his thinking and question his reasoning. If he's in a meeting he makes sure that everyone speaks, and he doesn't accept silence or complacency from anyone. He explained to me that as a leader he tries to make it clear to his colleagues that they are not trying to reach a common viewpoint. The goal is common action, not common thinking, and he expects his teams to disagree with him whenever they have a different opinion.

Duncan also uses another technique that I have found very helpful in certain situations. He will deliberately alter a single fact or assumption to see how that changes his team's approach to a problem. This enables leaders and their CPs to step back from the reality of a situation, in the hopes of refreshing their thinking. If you were using this in a business setting, you might ask: "We're assuming a 10 percent attrition rate in our customer base. What if that rate is 20 percent? How would our strategy change? What if it's 50 percent?" Others will choose to change many assumptions and create a fictional world to consider an issue. "Assume we are going to launch our product this year rather than next but at a cost structure 10 percent above what we believe we will be at and that our competition will be late but will cut price at its launch." Once it's understood that the discussion has moved into the realm of the hypothetical, where people can challenge their assumptions without risk, the creative juices really begin to flow.

This technique proved quite useful to me one time when I was consulting to a company that was planning to ramp up its mergers-and-acquisitions activity. They had a lot of cash on hand, and no shortage of opportunities to spend it, but the company had had no mandate for acquisitions in the recession, so the M&A group had grown rusty. Unused muscles atrophy quickly in an organization; people neglect to stay in shape for the day when things may change. I sat down with the M&A team and said, "Listen, I know this is going to be a little bit shocking to the system, but let's entertain the idea that you don't exist. What kind of function would we build for this corporation now? What would be the skills and the strategy?" Initially, the question shook them up a bit. You have to be respectful of the emotions you can trigger with this kind of speculation. Nonetheless, the little experiment produced exciting results. It liberated the members of the team, allowing them to articulate the world as they really saw it, without trying to shoehorn the facts into the work they were already doing. From there, we expanded the fiction in different directions, imagining the group with different resources at their disposal, or different personnel, or even a different mandate.

I often describe this process of changing a fact or creating a fiction as "probabilistic thinking," to differentiate from our more customary "binary thinking," which reduces too many complex issues to simplistic yes/no or good/bad questions. It's not that interest rates either stay the same or rise, but that they go up 1 percent or 2 percent or 3 percent; and then we debate the probability of these various moves. Changing the assumptions—changing the rules of the conversation—and assigning probabilities can produce amazingly creative and innovative ideas. However, this cannot happen until at least one, but ideally more, of the conversation partners has listened well enough and carefully enough to discern the inherent assumptions involved, and then formulated a conversation strategy that will get them all out on the table.

How might this look in a real business conversation? Michael Lewis, in *The Big Short*, his popular book about the financial crisis, explains how some interesting characters profited from going against the conventional wisdom of the financial industry. As I read the book, I couldn't help but think of how a hypothetical conversation, say, in 2007, between the CEO of a major financial company and one of her deputies (we'll call him Sam) might have gone. It's a broad-ranging discussion involving the company's strategic direction, and involves a fair amount of predictive forecasting about what the future of the economy and the financial industry will look like. Maybe Sam is talking through a plan to increase the size of the bank's securitization business, which is already generating huge profits for the company. For the purposes of our story, let's say that this unit is taking subprime mortgages and bundling them together into an instrument that was then sold on to outside investors. If the CEO was a good listener, and aware of the danger of holding near-certain assumptions, she might stop Sam and ask:

"You know, I see that this is a good plan, but what would have to change in the world around us to make it a bad plan? What would it take to change your opinion?"

Sam might stop for a moment to think, then say:

"Well, I guess if demand dried up we wouldn't want to be in the business of selling them . . . So far, demand for the paper has been going up and up with no sign of stopping, and we've just been assuming this will continue."

One core assumption uncovered. But the CEO keeps pressing:

"Okay, but what would make our customers stop demanding these synthetic securities? What are we assuming about the business environment that leads us to believe demand for the stuff is never-ending?"

Sam pauses again, then thinks out loud:

"Well, I guess an economic downturn—if the economy goes south, then the underlying assets will lose their value and the products we're selling will be worth less. Come to think of it, it wouldn't necessarily have to affect all the underlying assets—it could just affect a few of them or even just one category and that would make people skittish about any securitized products. I think it's a bit far-fetched but I guess it's always a possibility."

Again, the CEO is a good listener, so she has an appetite for this kind of out-loud thinking. Let's say she probes this topic a bit more, asking questions to help her and her CP better understand the more extreme scenario. "What do we think might cause the economy to decline? What is the probability associated with each of these scenarios?" The conversation then moves on to a discussion of the bank's balance sheet and exposure to risk. Eventually the subject of real estate pops up.

Sam: "So we do have a sizable amount of exposure to real estate. It's mostly through mortgage-backed securities and collateralized debt obligations, ones that we're either trying to sell or just holding to diversify our risk."

CEO: "Okay, and what kind of default rate are we anticipating?"

Sam: "Our models have a worst-case scenario of about 4 percent. With home prices going up like they are, it's hard to imagine it being any higher than that."

Immediately the CEO recognizes a status quo bias at work. She switches gears and goes from binary to probabilistic thinking.

CEO: "I have no doubt that your models are solid, Sam. But just for the sake of argument I want to lay out three hypothetical scenarios and then I want you to tell me what happens to our business and what our response would be. Let's say default rates go to 4 percent. What happens? Then, what happens at 7 percent? And, finally, let's assume Armageddon: house prices crash and default rates shoot up to 10 percent. How would that affect our business?"

The conversation progresses, and the CEO gains a great deal of insight, making her better able to respond when Armageddon ultimately does strike. Moreover, her deputy, Sam, comes out of the conversation with a whole different set of scenarios to contemplate. He doesn't necessarily change his assumptions right then and there. But by forcing him to test, defend, and amend them, the CEO made him better able to react when it became necessary. The executives might not have necessarily altered their business plan, but they would have developed some insights that would have made them more prepared when the moment for quick changes arrived. They would have ensured that they were not the frogs sitting sedately in the slowly boiling water.

Now, I admit that this conversation might sound a bit contrived. The idea is simply to illustrate how this kind of listening might work in real time, and to demonstrate how to spot assumptions and test them. The historical roots of the financial crisis were enormously deep, and spread in all directions. However, maybe a thousand such conversations in a number of companies and organizations, or academic and governmental corridors, could have prepared us a little bit better.

So we have arrived at what I believe to be a key secret of good listening: you must become the Master of the Question. Being the

Master of the Question means using questions to reframe the conversation in order to learn more. Through careful questioning we can open up new avenues of thinking by challenging or confirming our dearest assumptions.

It might sound impossible to remain so hypervigilant and coolly alert in every passing interaction, but don't let the simple idea of a more deliberate listening process intimidate you. You don't have to talk every last decision to death. Like playing scales on a piano, the mechanics will become second nature to you with time and with practice. It should never slow you down, or throw a wrench in your decision-making process. Approaching an assumption in the right manner from the outset will invariably save you time, and save you the effort of returning to problems and repeating previous mistakes. It will make you more efficient and more direct, increasing your chances of making good decisions and getting to right actions more quickly, and more reliably. Most importantly, because holding on to false or tired assumptions can be fatal to any organization, challenging them appropriately can make your career.

Keeping Your Focus

Every surgeon can look back on his residency as a kind of baptism by fire. I'm no exception. As a UCLA surgical resident I was doing a rotation at Martin Luther King Jr. hospital in the troubled Watts section of Los Angeles in the late 1970s. Victims of violence were not uncommon in MLK's emergency room, but one weekend stands out in my memory as particularly brutal. Patients began streaming into the hospital with gunshot and stab wounds on a Friday. Others had been beaten or injured in "vehicular mishaps." My team handled twenty surgical cases in the ensuing thirty-six-hour period. Think back to the waves of incoming wounded depicted on the old television series *M*A*S*H*, and you'll get a sense of what the hospital felt like that weekend.

While the scene in the hospital was one of barely controlled chaos—sirens and ambulances, doctors and nurses working on the run, police in riot gear patrolling corridors crowded with people still looking to finish their battles—inside the operating room, we worked with as much cool efficiency as we could muster. We had only one mission in mind: save the lives of the injured people in front of us. That meant tuning out anything and everything else that might clutter our brains or distract our attention. We needed to gather information, assess that information, and then choose action based on it, all as quickly as possible. If we were not fully "in the moment"—fully present with all our attention focused on the problems at hand—we could not make the decisions that would save lives. There was precious little margin for error: either we got it right, or we lost the patient.

I can't remember every detail of every case. Even at the time, we were so worried that we wouldn't remember who we had treated for what, that we wrote ourselves notes and reminders on their surgical bandages to prompt us later. I have memories of patients being wheeled in and out of the OR, and of having to instantly and totally force each prior case from my mind to make room for the next. I recall the strange sensation I had when we finished the last in this long siege of surgeries, as if the rest of the world came rushing suddenly back into my brain. It wasn't until we could all relax and take in everything that was going on around us that any of us understood how much we had been shutting out of our consciousness for so long.

Perhaps a trauma hospital is an extreme example of a work environment requiring single-minded focus. No doubt millions of others, from pilots landing airliners in storms, to short-order cooks during the lunch rush, to tennis players in the middle of a long, tense rally, have experienced that kind of all-consuming intensity. I have a friend who plays the banjo, and claims that hours can go by almost unnoticed while he's practicing his picking patterns, training his fingers through endless repetition. I've already referred to elite athletes getting "in the zone," in which time seems to slow down. They feel like they can see more, hear more, and quickly process information from multiple inputs with a unique interplay of instinct and heightened awareness. Pilots and cooks and musicians and surgeons can get in that zone as well. Experience develops muscle memory, so that in those moments, well-trained people don't need to focus on each movement or technique, but can focus on broader, or deeper, or more essential concerns.

The analogy to listening should be self-evident. It is a practicable skill, which will produce better results as your use of techniques to help you concentrate, and eliminate the distractions around you, becomes more automatic. Like any other skill, it becomes easier as you develop muscle memory. In the case of listening, the muscle in question is the one between your ears.

In an organizational setting, no less than in an operating room or on a flight deck, it is vital to keep one's focus, to isolate the problem or issue or decision at hand, and separate out any extraneous details or emotions that can reduce your ability to listen clearly and carefully. This kind of focus should be the goal for listening. Businessmen and -women deal with so many challenges and questions on any given day that it is easy to allow all that constant stream of mental activity to become a virtual cacophony swirling around inside their brains. Good listening demands that you cut out that white noise and focus on the conversation at hand. There will be times when you feel that an idea or problem is so important that you can't put it aside. However, it is never productive to expend more energy having an internal conversation than you're using to engage with your conversation partner. Oscar Wilde, the Irish poet, playwright, and novelist, commented on his own tendency to have brilliant conversations with himself; he didn't recommend it either. "I like hearing myself talk," he once said. "I often have long conversations all by myself, and I am so clever that sometimes I don't understand a single word of what I am saying." You already have enough distractions in your head.

Don't add to them by falling into Wilde's trap, dazzling yourself with your own cleverness. Not only might you fail to understand yourself, you most certainly will not hear a word of what your CP is saying.

In my effort to examine the art of listening as more of a craft, I've found it helpful to break the challenge of focusing into two components: the intellectual and the emotional. Turning first to the intellectual challenge, our ability to focus can be hindered by the many ongoing business projects and problems that are constantly overloading our thoughts. Managing all these external stimuli requires a process called *compartmentalizing.* If you are listening to a new product pitch but you're thinking about the performance review you will deliver to someone reporting to you, you'd be wasting your development team's time, and perhaps missing an important opportunity to listen.

I've observed a number of executives who have mastered the art of compartmentalizing. No matter how all-consuming one meeting or conversation might have been, they seemed always able to deal with that situation on its own terms, and then close the book on it, at least in the short term, so that they could address the next problem with equal focus. I recall sitting through a pair of meetings with the CEO of a technology company, early in my career. First, we huddled like a rugby scrum around a speakerphone, trying to bang out a complicated contract with a client. The terms were complex to the point of being labyrinthine, and I remember being bombarded by the clauses and caveats being added and subtracted in rapid succession. By the end of the phone meeting, it was clear that the deal was being fundamentally renegotiated. As a result, the CEO was now being forced to weigh a very different set of risks, which his company would have to manage under the new terms. A final decision was postponed to the next day. The countless bits of contractual minutiae were rattling around in my head, and the potential new risk weighed heavily on me, even though I was one step removed in my role as a consultant. I could only imagine how intensely the CEO was turning all this over in his mind.

I followed the CEO directly from that meeting to his office, where a team of investment bankers was waiting to negotiate the refinancing of some of the company's debt. We launched straight into it, running through scenarios and deal points as complex and unwieldy as the client contract had been. My head was spinning as the two deals almost started blurring into a single unmanageable tangle, but the CEO listened coolly, questioning and probing the bankers as if he were chatting about the next day's weather forecast. I was awed by his ability to compartmentalize, to put one set of problems on the shelf so that he could address another. His discipline and focus were remarkable.

As for the emotional component, a situation like the above can become even more complicated when our feelings and anxieties come into play. Imagine that the deal being renegotiated had determined the long-term survival of the organization and threatened the CEO's career. Or put yourself in the shoes of someone who is discussing some reorganization options with his boss that could effectively reduce that employee's own influence or authority. Would you be able to listen with an open mind and ask the questions that will generate a good decision under those circumstances? Suppose your desire to see a pet project succeed prevents you from hearing colleagues discuss its inherent obstacles. Could you filter your emotional support out of the conversation?

Any number of other emotional responses can come between you and your conversation partner. *Decoupling* is the term I've assigned to the process of separating your emotions from the substance of the conversation. Haven't you found yourself listening to someone talk while thinking, "Oh, get on with it already! Get to the point!" Or maybe, "We've been over this already; you're saying the same thing you said five minutes ago, except in different words!" Before you know it, those feelings of *impatience* can turn you into an Opinionator or an Answer Man. You're so eager to move the conversation forward that you start interrupting in nonproductive ways, finishing your CP's thoughts just to get to the next step. Your impatience might not even have anything to do with your CP, but may be related to the next item on your agenda, or a looming deadline that seems to get closer with every meandering turn the conversation takes.

Emotions like resentment or jealousy can also impede good listening. But perhaps the most pernicious negative emotion is *threat*, in all its forms. If you're feeling threatened in a conversation or encounter, you won't be able to process the information properly. All you will hear is the threat, and you are likely to miss things that could have an impact on whatever decisions you need to make. Just as the Department of Homeland Security posts a range of "threat levels" and alerts, individuals deal with a continuum of threats. On the lower end of the spectrum, we perceive threats to our status or reputation, and become reflexively defensive. In conversation, we're so busy framing arguments to justify ourselves, that we can no longer be "in the moment," with our attention focused on listening.

The threat we feel can progress through different levels of intensity, up to the point of real fear. Even the most rudimentary management training teaches that when rating an employee's performance, the reviewer should never open with something negative. We know that once you've put something on the table that a person can perceive as a threat, it will become his entire focus, and anything else you say may fall on deaf ears. It's impossible to listen when you feel like there's a gun pointed at your head.

Positive emotions can be just as treacherous as negative ones.

Perhaps some big idea comes to light in the course of conversation, causing everyone involved to burst into excited chatter about all the possibilities. For a moment, you're flush with optimism as new ideas come spilling out. But beware: a high level of *excitement*, just like anger or fear, can distract you from asking the right questions, from probing deeper, or from examining and challenging the underlying assumptions of the discussion.

Sometimes a subject simply wears you out. Perhaps you find yourself in one too many sessions to explore cost control. Maybe you've been sitting too long tossing back and forth the same solutions to the same intractable problems. Mental fatigue and frustration— two sides of the same coin—can take your head out of a conversation as effectively as any other emotion. The simple fact is that anything that prevents you from remaining fully present in a conversation keeps you from listening effectively. I had a colleague once, an astute and successful individual, who had a strange and occasionally infuriating habit of "checking out," right in the middle of a meeting, or even during a one-on-one conversation. He would just retreat into daydream, or let his mind wander to some other topic that had caught his attention. You could see it in his eyes and hear it in his manner if you were paying enough attention. I used to joke with him about it. "Hey!" I'd say, trying to bring him back to earth. "Is it nice where you go?" We'd laugh about it, but the point is that it didn't matter whether or not it was nice where he went. Wherever it was, it was a location from which he had ceased listening.

Nobody likes to think of him or herself as being able to strip emotion out of all interactions. We may all admire *Star Trek*'s Mr. Spock, but nobody really wants to *be* Mr. Spock, at least not all the time. We don't want to be perceived as cold or callous or mechanical. But there are circumstances in which we must realize that to function most effectively, we need to decouple from our emotions. Let's go back to that marathon weekend of surgery all those years ago. My job—my *only* job—was to treat those patients as well as I could. It wouldn't do the patient on the table any good to have my head filled with worry about their families out in the waiting room, or some issue in my own career. Likewise, anyone who has tough problems to confront can't stop to worry about the emotional ramifications at every turn. You have to see clearly the facts in front of you that can contribute to good decisions and good actions.

Consider military training. Sure, you have to accumulate a new knowledge base, and learn how to think in different ways, but an enormous part of this kind of training is designed to re-create the live conditions of combat. Trainees are deliberately inured to those conditions, so that by the time they have to function under them, the external circumstances can recede into the background rather than occupy too much of their attention.

As I matured as a businessperson I found that the conditions surrounding a problem were less concerning to me than the problems themselves. I grew calmer, less distracted, and more able to compartmentalize and to decouple—to focus. It felt to me that, as my comfort level and confidence increased, time essentially slowed down the higher the stakes were. I was able to listen better, take in and process more information, communicate more effectively, and arrive at better, quicker decisions that led to more productive action. I became better at what I did.

I can hear you grumbling, "Am I supposed to become a Zen master now? Just will myself to tune out the world and focus on whatever little thing is in front of me?" True, it's one thing to describe an ideal, but that doesn't make it easy to achieve. Believe me, I don't expect anyone to become some kind of perfect listening machine.

Think of the advice and action steps I lay out as signposts along the way to that ideal. If none of us ever quite gets to that destination, at least we can make steady progress.

Some days I sit in meetings or have conversations in which I know I'm distracted and I have to face the fact that I'm compromised as a conversation partner. Clearly, these conversations are less likely to get anyone where they need to go. Everyone should expect this to happen from time to time; it's natural, and it doesn't represent a failure on anybody's part. Be honest with yourself when this is happening, and take steps to correct the situation.

The simplest, but at the same time the most extreme, step you can take is the rip-cord approach—bail out and pull the cord on your parachute. If you realize that you just can't get yourself to focus enough to be of value to your CP, the wisest course may be to put the conversation off to a time when you can better get your head in the game—if circumstances allow. It may strike you as rude to tell someone that you want to end a conversation because you're too distracted or unable to focus, but, on the contrary, I believe it shows respect for your conversation partners to let them know that you don't want to waste their valuable time. The rip-cord option won't always be available to you; some conversations can't wait, and sometimes, social rhythms or concerns about organizational etiquette prevent you from abandoning a conversation. In those cases, you will need to carry on, acknowledging to yourself that your focus is reduced.

What can you do to get your head back into the game when bailing out isn't an option? There are a few simple techniques that have worked for me. Recall that early on, I referred to a kind of duality of consciousness. Buddhists use the term "mindfulness" to describe the quality of being fully "in the moment." At the same time, it is possible to step outside yourself and, in effect, observe yourself experiencing that moment. I sometimes play a game with myself when I'm distracted, where I imagine that the conversation is being filmed for a movie. We're on a set, and I assume the role of director in my mind. This little fiction makes me step back from the conversation and consider what the scene is about, who the characters are and what's really being said. Sure, you could say that this technique is a form of purposeful distraction, but in fact it can bring the key elements of the conversation into sharper definition. It slows down the conversation, quiets your mind, and pushes out other distracting noise.

You can also try to gain focus by remembering that a good listener is the Master of the Question. Set yourself the goal of distilling the various elements of the conversation into one killer question, like the "killer app" that turns a new device into a necessity. The killer question is like a great listener's magic bullet, the question that refocuses both you and your CP. The goal of coming up with that killer question can be a powerful force for focusing your listening. You'll think more critically about the information coming your way, directing your mind to the here and now, rather than letting it dwell on the problem you left on the last conference room table.

On some occasions, I've returned to an old-fashioned device to make myself concentrate: taking notes. This isn't my favorite technique, partly because I sometimes find note-taking by others to be distracting. I confess that it makes me wonder if they're really listening well, if they are focused on recording what we're saying, rather than on engaging and processing more naturally. I'll never forget one man I worked with who had mastered the curious art of taking notes without ever breaking his eye contact with his CP. Ironically, I found this skill of his even more distracting, because all I could think was, "How does he do that?" I've known some people who didn't take notes during a meeting or conversation but would jot down a few key phrases as soon as the encounter ended. This approach may constitute the best of both worlds. Either way, jotting down a few notes can be a useful short-term tool in helping you concentrate on what's being said.

Each of these three techniques forces you to step back from a conversation and identify the fundamental issues and questions at hand. By taking you outside the conversation, these steps can help you find your way back into it. They lower the static in your head so that you can be the finely tuned and proactive listener you need to be. We've already established that good listening requires you to be participatory. Allowing yourself to be distracted is, in a sense, the very height of passivity. My experience is that it is much easier to focus when you take positive action to engage. The techniques that work for me may not work for you, but remember this basic idea: when you've lost your focus and have fallen into the traps of poor listening, ask yourself how you can start listening with a different set of ears.

Most of the managers I've worked with have built their ability to focus on the job gradually over time. But a few have had experiences in life that sped their learning along. Two stand out in my mind. One was a Catholic nun who ran a sizable health-care system in the Pacific Northwest. Whenever her world started to get really chaotic she became ever more serene. One evening at a management retreat she and I were sitting alone in a bar, each of us enjoying a tumbler of Jameson whiskey. I asked her how she reached this calm state of concentration when the entire world around her seemed like it was losing its mind. She smiled, lifted her eyebrows heavenward, and said: "I've got a helper."

Another executive whom I admired for her focus and equanimity replied to the same question by saying: "I have four children at home. No matter what happens at work, by comparison it's a lot less stressful than the chaos at home. I tell you, those kids have trained me pretty well!" To me, that just said it all.

You are now equipped with the essential tools of Power Listening:

respecting your conversation partner, keeping quiet, challenging assumptions, and staying focused. As you master these techniques, you will find that you amass a great wealth of information and ideas. And the better you become at listening, the more this wealth will grow. Now the challenge becomes how to manage this wealth of information and put it to work for you.

SECTION

TWO

Sorting the Chaos

Now that I've explained the basic tools of Power Listening it's time to develop techniques for harnessing what you hear in service of a leaner and better-informed decision-making process. This involves:

▶ Identifying what a conversation is all about

▶ Capturing the information that matters from any conversation or meeting

▶ Steering a conversation in order to ensure that you gather all that information

▶ Knowing how to sort and process the information received

▶ Filing away the information so you can remember, recall, and use it when necessary

At this point, you're well grounded in the understanding of listening as an active process, in which you take steps to improve and expand what you know. I've already established that any great listener must become the Master of the Question. Indeed, questions are the key to this part of the listening process. They are your ticket to staying actively engaged and the tool you use to get all those facts and pieces of data that you need to solve your business problems. The system I introduce in this chapter is one designed to help you determine the kind of questions you ought to be asking—and then where to file that information away once you receive it. I want to help you build an information framework. It will assist you in developing the right questions and will allow you to sift and sort and classify the chaotic rush of incoming information, so that you can apply it to your decision making and get to actions that make a difference.

Why do I make such a big deal about constructing an information framework that will work for you? Simple: conversations focused on critical business issues can be enormously complicated. Sometimes conversations will be so scattershot that you will need a listening system just to place the conversation in its appropriate context. You will need to figure out how to keep things straight, to help you process and remember information. It can be helpful to keep a guide in your head that allows you to formulate the next important question, so that you can fill in any critical gaps and make sure that you have every necessary fact when it comes time to make a call.

When I think about this framework I picture a set of file drawers representing the broad categories of business problem solving and action. The categories that work for me are *mandate, plan, team, execution,* and *personal*. These are broad and general categories that together are comprehensive enough to cover most of the issues that managers face. Conversations in business will almost always be about one or more of these topics. I offer these rather general categories as a possible framework for your listening, and do not intend them to substitute for the detailed theory and effort that goes into making strategy and managing organizations. I am only trying to lay out an inventory of overarching concerns that can translate into the file drawers you might use to organize your listening. If this discussion whets your appetite for a more serious exploration of strategy and management theories, the libraries and bookstores are filled to bursting with valuable literature.

These file drawers help me to keep track of where I ought to store the information I hear, as well as which questions still remain to be asked. Within those categories I also imagine file folders representing the more specific issues that are likely to be relevant to the major labels listed above. They will include such diverse topics as metrics, timing, risk, organizational wherewithal, skill sets, and so on.

These file folders and the drawers they fill form the basis for my personal system of deliberate, active listening. They may not be the same drawers and folders that you would use, which is only natural. Most seasoned businesspeople will have developed a unique set of preferences and devised their own system of relevant categories and questions. In fact, some managers I know think about their systems of organization somewhat differently. For example, Daniel Vasella, the Novartis Chairman, visualizes a road map when he is in a conversation and uses that map to steer through the discussion and get from the big picture and overview to the places that require elucidation and clarification. If you choose file drawers as your system, there will likely be matters of great importance to you that are absolutely unique to your enterprise. There will also be bolts from the blue, surprise issues you could not have anticipated. As singular as some of these events or concerns may seem, they can provide learning opportunities, and so have lasting value. Any time you have to create a new file drawer or folder, it stays there, providing an additional question in your arsenal that can deepen your understanding of future situations. In the course of my development as a focused listener, I have needed to add folders, perhaps for new regulatory issues, or for risk associated with volatile parts of the world, or unanticipated social trends or cultural resistance.

Like so many other aspects of active listening, the process will sound complicated, and maybe even cumbersome to you, but it will grow easier and more natural with time. The more you go back to your file drawers and folders, the more automatically the questions will form themselves in your mind during conversations, and the more quickly you'll be able to surface the kind of information you need to spur positive action.

Lastly, you will notice that the chapters in this section are all geared toward making sure that people in conversations are working with common purpose toward unified action. That is to say, a certain level of agreement on mandate or plan or execution is critical to people working together in a company or an organization. But of course, there are conversations in business where this isn't the case. Sometimes, the person sitting across the table from you is a competitor, or perhaps a customer or supplier whose mandate is diametrically opposed to yours, and the conversation may be adversarial or even hostile. You might even find yourself up against someone in your own organization who has it in for you for some reason, or who sees things very differently from you. It's my belief that the techniques I describe here can be just as useful to you in these settings. If you listen intently to an adversarial CP you can still use your file drawers to sort and process the information you're hearing. The difference in working with an adversarial CP is that coordination and getting on the same page are not the objectives. If you believe the old saying, "keep your friends close and your enemies closer," as I do, this is a practice you cannot do without.

It goes without saying that the challenges facing each company or organization in any given industry or pursuit are going to be unique. I don't expect that the file drawers or file folders I propose will fit your situation precisely. Nor can I provide a complete business education to inform your thinking or problem solving. But I do want to provide a basic scheme from which you can tailor your own bespoke system. What I present is a sampler of some of the questions I have found useful in a broad range of conversations. If I'm successful with this part of the book you will emerge with your own set of file drawers, folders, and questions that will allow you to make better sense of the chaos that comes at you in your daily listening.

What Is the Mandate?

I was traveling with a top executive from a major communications company at a time when that industry was going through some seismic changes. I was listening to him tell me about how he was questioning the company's future economic viability. I say I was listening, but it had been a long week. We were supposed to be having a Friday evening drink to wind down, and given how many times I had heard him express these concerns, I was frankly not paying too much attention. Then, alarm bells went off in my head as he said, "Why in the hell does this company have to exist?" I knew that my week hadn't really ended. We spent the next few hours concluding that indeed, the company didn't need to exist. Time and the marketplace had passed it by, at least in its current form. As you might imagine, that insight took our discussion in a whole new direction. The company would survive, but not before it rethought its most basic business assumptions, and eventually remade itself and its aspiration to fit into a new market reality.

The Secretary of Education, Arne Duncan, says he is always

listening carefully to teachers, principals, parents, and politicians to discover whether they share his aspirations for improving primary and secondary education. I admire Duncan as a listener. Can you imagine the challenges he faces in addressing what many argue is the largest strategic threat to the United States, its declining position in the world's educational rankings? Wherever the secretary goes, emotions run high. Whether he's speaking with students or parents, educators or politicians, conversations are often tense, and frustration often boils over. Americans love to play the blame game, particularly regarding education. Duncan has heard all the rationalizations and explanations—teachers' unions, poor parenting, too much TV—but he listens hardest for aspirations. If he can discern an aspiration that aligns with his own, he latches on to it, no matter how confrontational that conversation is. In Secretary Duncan's world, at the volatile intersection of education and politics, finding common ground among the many stakeholders may be the biggest challenge of all. His commitment to unearthing the aspirations that can form the basis of a shared mandate has earned him a reputation as a "consensus listener."

Most of the conversations you have in the work environment won't overtly confront such cosmic questions as whether a company should exist or how to improve education in the United States, but you would probably be surprised how often problem solving in business can be derailed by a simple misperception or misalignment about the *mandate* of an organization. What is the company's basic purpose? Its essential mission? Why are we all here? You might think that this kind of question only concerns CEOs and others at the highest levels of management. Not so. In fact, I would go so far as to say that the most common factor I've witnessed in business failures is a lack of agreement about the company's mandate throughout the workforce. Think about it: A salesperson wants to keep a major customer happy and finds savings opportunities by trimming the features of his company's product. He sees lowering the price to keep the customer's business as priority number one. That sales manager has prioritized market share, understandably believing that to be his mandate. But what if the corporation's mandate was to be first in engineering and to pursue a more niche strategy, offering a more sophisticated product with higher margins to fewer customers? The salesperson's decision to sacrifice a level of product feature in favor of customer volume could be very damaging in a larger context.

All the parties involved in a business conversation must work toward agreeing on the company's mandate, or appreciating that there are multiple mandates at work. Everybody needs to be able to answer a few fundamental questions: What does this company stand for? Why do we value that? Why should we? I believe that if you listen to how your CP answers these questions for himself, and hear that your answers are in alignment, you've set the stage for a fruitful conversation. Whenever I think about mandate, I recall fondly that Catholic nun running a large medical delivery system in the northwest United States. If there were more than a few people in the room for a meeting, she would always begin by asking everyone to observe a moment of silence and remind them that they were there to care for the sick and protect the healthy. She would then sit silently for about forty-five seconds before beginning the conversation. Powerful stuff!

Think back on the most important business conversations you have had over the last month. Would they have been more productive if you had listened first for clues to the essential mandate with which your CP was working? I've learned that regardless of whom I'm speaking with, or the nature of our conversation, I have to keep focused, tuned in for anything that reveals what my CP believes his or her organization stands for. This context will enable me to get the most out of what my CP is saying.

Here, I'm talking about big aspirations, not short-term goals or milestones. When I ask about mandates, I hear some answers that are too obvious on their face. When a CEO says to me, "My mandate is to increase shareholder value," or "I want my earnings to be $3.50 per share," I know I'm not at the right level of discussion. In that situation, I need to focus on discovering the stars the company reaches for, the ones that exist outside the daily grind of targets and metrics, the stretch goals that likely defy the odds of success as understood today.

Here are a few mandates I've heard that might give you a better idea of what I mean. The CEO of a large urban children's hospital tells me, "I'd like never to lose another child to cancer again." An executive running a remote diagnostic and maintenance operation says, "I want to eliminate any downtime of our equipment." "We become the number one competitor in China ahead of the home-grown, government-funded alternative," says the CEO of a multinational based in Europe. Each of these mandates, although profoundly ambitious, is also concrete enough to trigger specific action, even if a radical innovation or strategic breakthrough is needed to fulfill that ambition. Moreover, these actions inspired by the mandate will likely be more challenging than the goals that most people deal with every day, involving longer time frames and requiring resources that either don't exist, or are currently in short supply within the organization.

Mandate discussions can be brief and much more specific than the grand, open-ended conversations triggered by a question like, "Why does the company exist?" Without doubt, however, agreement about the answers to those big questions should inform each nitty-gritty discussion. Whatever level you are working at in the organization, it's important to make sure you and the CP see success exactly alike. You may have to be a pest about getting to that shared understanding; it can be uncomfortable to define a vague mandate or to reshape one. You shouldn't be surprised if this process becomes taxing at times, nor should you underestimate its absolute necessity.

Some years ago, I was consulting to a company based in an emerging market to help them reach their stated aspiration of doubling growth in the next five years. This company had a first-rate product set and CEO. I recommended ways for the company to upshift its unique line of products and bring in talent from all over the globe to supercharge that growth. I couldn't imagine a better plan for turning the company into an international force, but for some reason the CEO and his executives kept resisting my ideas. Now, I've learned over the years that when people resist, they've probably got a good reason, and after going back and forth with them for the better part of an hour, I figured out where the disconnect lay. I had been assuming their mandate was to conquer the world. Instead, the group only wanted to further dominate their backyard. Obviously, those are two very different goals, requiring different strategies. It turns out that the more modest mandate was the right one for the company, which was one-third owned by the government. They knew that home-country contracts would be theirs for the taking, and would never go to their foreign competitors. With an obvious home-field advantage, their smartest move was to capitalize on and to continue to develop their competitive edge in their local market, at least in the shorter term. Imagine how much more productive our time could have been if we had been clear on that mandate from the start.

So, let me offer some practical tips for uncovering your CP's understanding of mandate in a conversation. Remember that my technique for ensuring that I gather the necessary and appropriate information during a conversation is to imagine a set of file drawers. Each drawer contains folders labeled with questions that reflect the critical subcategories of information. As my CP talks, I listen closely for any bits of information that I can slot easily into one of the folders. If those bits don't seem to be naturally forthcoming, I can simply ask the questions that appear on the folders. It's more cumbersome to fill all the folders in a single stand-alone conversation than as part of an ongoing dialogue with a colleague over a period of time. If I have numerous conversations with a CP, I may not bring up all, or even any, of these questions in any one conversation, if I already have what I need for that encounter. But I always keep those folders open in my head, to remind me of what I'm seeking. I really don't want to relive the experience of being on a different page from everyone else in the room because of a misunderstood mandate.

Here are the questions that appear on the file folders in my "Mandate" drawer:

Question 1. Why are we here?

This is a fundamental question, but a practical, not a metaphysical one. What are the enduring, overarching aspirations? What is the fundamental reason for being? On what does the organization base its identity? This is where you have to start. Use this question or your version of it to ensure that you and any conversation partner have a shared understanding of the group's mandate. Get clarity here, at this level of abstraction, and then proceed to the other questions.

I have always found it valuable to fill this folder as early as possible. For instance, I remember a company that was cited by a regulatory body for quality issues. The initial reflex reaction was to say,

"Let's figure out how to get out of this for the least amount of money." The management team debated the options, going round and round during a series of intense but somehow unsatisfactory discussions, until one executive stepped back from the fray and started asking some basic questions. As soon as questions like "What are we doing here?" and "What do we think we stand for?" were on the table, the conversation gelled, as the team reconnected with and reaffirmed the company's fundamental mandate: to be a standard-bearer for quality. The strategy that grew out of that process allowed the company to create extraordinary new quality-control measures that would reset the bar for the industry. What a difference a mandate can make.

Question 2: Are there any misalignments?

Any lack of alignment or acceptance of a mandate can have disastrous consequences for a company or organization. More than one major corporation has suffered in this way, squandering both time and resources. I would argue that U.S. car companies' recent troubles could be traced to a lack of alignment on their mandate over a long period of time. These companies seemed to be pulled in many directions, with little coordination between management and labor, or, for that matter, *within* management and labor. As a result the companies were nearly brought to their knees.

Perhaps it seems overly simplistic to portray the troubles of the automotive industry purely in terms of mandate. One could argue that it was not the absence of a mandate, but rather a surplus of mandates, that caused the problem. Each stakeholder group—labor, management, shareholders, suppliers and retailers, not to mention customers and regulators—may have had clarity about its own goals and aspirations, but there was no unity and no alignment between those individual mandates. In the real world, this is going to be the case more often than not. The best leaders listen to and monitor, and then manage, the complicated interplay of conflicting mandates, a fluid phenomenon that requires ongoing attention and regular reassessment. The dynamic tension generated by the multiple mandates of different stakeholders provides grist for the mandate discussion again and again, and can produce richer, more beneficial shared mandates when managed thoughtfully.

Questions of mandate become even more complex and interesting when one considers how a mandate aligns with external factors, like a changing marketplace or a volatile economy. Businesses and organizations need to remain flexible, to know when their articulated mandate doesn't make sense in new conditions. Mandates in business are not written in stone, nor do they come from a higher authority. A wonderful illustration of this is IBM, a company that completely remade itself after revising its mandate to fit a new competitive environment. After years of supplying big-box computers to business, the company got a sharp wake-up call in the 1980s from its customers, who no longer needed IBM machines when they realized they could get comparable equipment at lower cost from a growing contingent of Asian manufacturers. Recognizing that their homegrown hardware business offered them a shrinking competitive advantage, IBM began working with a new mandate—to provide computing *services* rather than just computing *machines*. It aligned itself around a new fundamental imperative: offer custom, designed, or outsourced information services to customers, and if that happens to facilitate some hardware sales, all the better. IBM discovered the need to amend its historical mandate by listening to loyal customers. The company was able to revise its business model, reclaim customers, and develop new ones, at higher profit margins than in the past. The company not only survived a grave competitive challenge, it thrived.

Question 3: Can we work with this mandate?

It's one thing for a mandate to be inspiring on an emotional or intellectual level, but it also has to be practical. It must fertilize planning and execution. There are three component questions you need to answer to fill up this particular file folder:

▶ *Does the mandate capture the imagination and energy of the leadership team?* That is to say, does it reflect the best thinking and best intentions of the top people in the company?

▶ *Can the mandate be communicated more broadly to all the stakeholders?* A mandate that is overly esoteric or subtle or multilayered will be open to conflicting interpretations, no matter how carefully it is articulated, thus exacerbating the very problems a mandate should resolve.

▶ *Can the mandate be translated into a plan?* An organization can benefit from alignment around a clear mandate only if the aspirations represented by that mandate can be made operational.

I was fortunate to witness these principles in action when I was advising a major U.S. defense contractor that needed to move quickly to reduce costs and improve profit margins. Developments both within and outside the United States had caused upheaval in their industry, and they had pressing concerns about their financial health. I recall sitting in a meeting of the company's CEO and the top eight executives, listening to them propose a series of conflicting or half-baked ideas to address their lagging competitive position. After four unproductive hours, the meeting broke up for lunch. The executives couldn't seem to agree on anything, and everyone was worn out and frustrated. When we had a minute alone, the CEO turned to me and said, "I feel like we've forgotten what we're here for: To keep this country safe." The comment might have come across as somewhat unhelpful in the face of rather urgent pressures. But when the group reassembled after lunch, the CEO opened by reminding them of that lofty purpose, and very quickly galvanized the discussion. It was as if a switch was flipped. The executives began to better formulate their ideas. The changing dynamics of the group allowed those ideas to take the shape of a practical plan that would lead not only to immediate cost control, but also to a rigorous and comprehensive reassessment of their product development and manufacturing productivity.

• • •

If you see the opportunity in your conversation, attend to the questions in the "Mandate" file drawer. As we move now to the questions that make up the other, more concrete file drawers, I hope you will see how a misalignment of mandate can corrupt conversations involving other categories.

What Is the Plan?

Every business that seeks to improve its performance needs a plan to realize its mandate. Mandate is the destination, but without a well-drawn plan for getting there, even the most finely chiseled mandate becomes just an amalgam of moonbeams and vapors. A thoughtful and workable plan is formed and amended through many conversations about how to move forward. The headline question for a plan is simple: "What are you going to do now?"

In this chapter, we'll tease this basic question apart, using our system of file drawers and folders to organize the category into basic component questions that can be used to better explain any plan issue. These questions will help you as you listen to identify when your CP is talking about a plan and to sort that information into the appropriate file folders.

A few years ago, a good friend of mine—an experienced and successful entrepreneur by the name of Charles—spoke with me about an idea for taking his business in a new direction. Charles was in what's colloquially known as the "rag trade." He owned a high-end men's clothing retailer in one of America's smaller cities. His two stores harked back to a time before national department-store chains and big-box retailers, when familiar, locally owned retailers were the commercial anchors at the center of most American communities. Charles's business was a fixture in his hometown, with a solid base of long-standing customers who relied on his impeccable fashion sense and personalized service. Like so many talented retailers of his ilk, Charles rarely purchased stock for his stores without already feeling certain that a good 80 percent of it would be quickly snapped up by his regular clientele.

Charles knew men's clothing inside and out, and when thinking about ways to keep his business healthy and growing in a changing economy, he hit upon an idea for expanding the operation that would provide a direct benefit to his base of loyal customers. He would vertically integrate, by acquiring a suit-manufacturing firm. He could create a product line for sale in his own stores, as well as through the network of similar outlets in other cities, all of which he knew very well. Charles's decision coincided with an acquisition opportunity: an established independent manufacturer in another country was being put up for sale by its owners.

Given that he was considering a major undertaking, our conversation ranged over a wide variety of topics, but as we talked, I realized that many of the issues that he had put on the table fell into one of the folders in my "Plan" drawer. That awareness helped me focus my listening, and allowed me to guide my friend in sorting out his thinking and making grounded decisions about how to proceed. The first folder in the "Plan" drawer that I generally seek to fill, and then to update as appropriate, concerns the concrete objectives that form the backbone of any plan.

Question 1: What are the specific objectives that begin to move a company toward its mandate?

A mandate is by nature aspirational, and often somewhat blurry around the edges. The initial step toward fulfilling such a mandate is to begin making it more real and practical, by defining specific tangible objectives that incorporate that aspiration into the ongoing efforts of the organization. These objectives should represent important wins along what can be a long journey toward a mandate.

My friend Charles's mandate in this situation was indeed aspirational—his ideas, not just about the fashions themselves, but about marketing, packaging, and merchandising his goods, would represent a quiet revolution in men's shopping habits. Making this vision a reality required some well-defined objectives.

His first objective was to complete the purchase of the suit manufacturer, and then integrate it smoothly into his ongoing operation. The second objective was to reposition his brand—to bring about a shift in the public image of his business, not just with his existing customer base, but also in the other retail outlets that he needed to secure to market and sell his new clothing line.

There are two components to the Objectives question: First, we listen for how the objectives contemplated by the CP are aligned with the mandate. Then we listen for the clarity of the objectives, and carefully consider the process that generated them. I try to ascertain whether, when the decision was made, those responsible had covered all their bases, asked all the right questions, and been able to glean the most thoughtful, complete, honest, and accurate information from everyone involved. When Charles made it clear that he had set himself the objective of acquiring the manufacturing operation,

I was sure that the planned move was driven directly by the mandate, but that was not to say that it was the only available move. Was it possible, for instance, to purchase the goods—designed and manufactured according to his own specifications—from a third party, and sell them under his own private label? I listened carefully as Charles described how he had explored that option but discovered that the possible alternatives at the time afforded him neither the control he desired nor the quality he sought.

As the owner-operator of a relatively small company, Charles didn't require the agreement of a board of directors or a large management hierarchy to set the objective of acquiring the manufacturer. In some larger organizations, the very process of securing the buy-in of all the relevant parties can put a plan on the wrong track. I read Jerry Harvey's book, *The Abilene Paradox*, a number of years ago, and can approach any conversation, especially those that concern planning, with the benefit of his insight. Professor Harvey's book opens with a story of a day trip he took with his wife and in-laws from Coleman, Texas, to have dinner in a cafeteria in Abilene. Harvey's father-in-law had proposed the trip primarily to get everyone out of the house and liven up a stultifying July night. One by one, each family member bought into the plan. They piled into the family's 1958 Buick and headed out into the 104-degree Texas night with no air-conditioning. By the time they got home, sweaty and miserable and grousing about the bad food at the Abilene restaurant, they were all wondering why they had ever left the comfort of home in the first place. There was some finger-pointing, to be sure, but they quickly figured out that each one had agreed to make the trip mostly because they thought it was what the others wanted to do, even though none of them individually thought it was a good idea.

Professor Harvey called this phenomenon the Abilene paradox:

People manage to come together in agreement on an objective—in this case traveling to Abilene—that no one actually believes is the right one. One characteristic of the Abilene paradox is: "Organizational members fail to accurately communicate their desires and/or beliefs to one another. In fact, they do just the opposite, thereby leading one another into misperceiving the collective [objective]." The bad decision they made can be traced directly to the lack of clarity and agreement about the objective, but just as important, to a lack of openness and directness in their communication. Harvey's research revealed that companies find themselves in this situation largely because of inadequate communication, and that means poor listening as much as it means people failing to express themselves clearly. People respond ambiguously or tentatively to proposals they don't fully support, maybe to hedge their bets, maybe to cover their backsides or avoid rocking the boat, or maybe because they're honestly not confident in their own judgment. Executives go along with what they think are misguided schemes because they want to look like team players, or they don't want to cross their boss, or let down a colleague. Their conversation partners, if they aren't listening with focus and with purpose, are likely to hear only what they want to hear, guaranteeing a flawed decision-making process.

When enough people sign on to a plan or an objective just to placate other parties in a conversation or within the organization—or for any other wrong reason—you end up with the worst possible result: an organization forging ahead with a plan that nobody believes in. There's no surer way to take a costly detour away from the shared mandate. Of course, it's just a parable, but in the real world, a focused listener who questions assumptions and takes nothing for granted can avoid these traps. The lesson from Abilene is to spend the time listening to what objectives exist, challenging them for their relevance to the mandate, demanding candor and full disclosure from every CP, and assuring yourself and others that everyone truly sees the shared objectives as the correct ones.

Question 2: What are the specific initiatives that will help achieve the objectives?

This may seem pretty obvious on its face, but be prepared to be surprised. As I talk about mandates, objectives, and now initiatives, understand that I am referring to a hierarchy of specificity, or granularity. In the case of the clothier Charles, for instance, the initiatives included negotiating the purchase of the foreign company and securing the financing for the deal. Our conversation brought to light the fact that Charles would have to develop initiatives—concrete action steps—to find his way through a complex regulatory maze; his status as a "foreign buyer" raised a new set of hurdles. Then, he needed to redirect the actual design and manufacturing operations within the newly acquired company to fit with his own plan. The key concept to understand is that steps must be described and understood in more practical detail the nearer you approach the time of actual execution.

I am ruthlessly exacting when it comes to listening and questioning about initiatives. I've been known to gently hammer away at CPs until I hear them talk about initiatives with a level of completeness that's appropriate, and until they've laid out a direct connection between the initiative, the objective, and the mandate. What I'm really sensitive to is whether there is wasted motion. You would be wise to enter into conversations about planned initiatives with the presumption that they are likely to be too complicated or too numerous to be manageable. While listening for individual initiatives that are clear and simple and easy to communicate, a good litmus test is that the aggregate of initiatives undertaken by an organization add up to a plan that is both credible and achievable.

Question 3: What is the timeline?

If there is one thing that managers have the most trouble anticipating and predicting, it's pace. Planners and strategists in business need to challenge the timeline rigorously. When it comes to timing, I find I need to take my *active* listening approach and kick it up a notch, to where you could almost describe it as *aggressive* listening. Challenge the underpinnings by pointed questioning until you understand the complete sequence of events related to an objective or initiative, including relevant contingencies. Charles and I ran through the numbers, and were able to determine that he would need to have the re-tooled manufacturing operation up and running within one year if his plan was to be financially viable. Once that timeline was out on the table, we could go back and analyze each piece of the plan, add them all together, and decide whether or not the date could be met.

Fill this file folder until it's bursting, if necessary; it's the only way to schedule and sequence any plan with confidence. It will help you pay particular attention to milestones along the way. Are you and your CP in agreement about how often, and by what standards, you will mark your progress, in order to maintain confidence in your schedule?

If you have any doubts about how easy it is to miscalculate timelines, imagine trying to book a flight on a Boeing 787 Dreamliner in 2008, when it was supposed to be flight-ready but still hadn't left the ground. What about Boston's "Big Dig," the massive highway and tunnel project intended to reroute traffic through the heart of the city, in which the endless construction delays were matched only by the monumental cost overruns? And the next time you're in New York, see if you can take a ride on the Second Avenue subway line, which has been on the planning boards for at least seventy-five years, and at this point is a great big hole in the ground.

Question 4: What assets are required, and are they available?

This question will emerge again when we talk about the Team and Execution file drawers, but for the purpose of my Plan drawer I always say to myself: "Okay, if I'm going to shoot at a target, do I have a gun, the ammo, and by the way, can I even shoot?" These questions regarding assets themselves are simple and straightforward, but when asked in a business-plan setting the answers can involve a dizzying array of factors.

Different types of initiatives require different types of assets to ensure that you keep momentum and get to the finish line successfully. I won't attempt to give you a list of all the assets you should consider, but instead I will give you a place to start. Let me suggest an often-used distinction between tangible and intangible assets. Examples of the former can include: factories and warehouses, equipment, capital, or numbers (as opposed to types) of people. Intangible assets can include capabilities, mind-sets, information, and key relationships.

The tangible assets related to Charles's plan were easy to spot. Most obviously, the company he wanted to purchase was a good one, on solid footing, with years of experience and a reputation for productivity and dependability. Secondly, he had already begun speaking to potential backers, and had reasonable confidence that the financing would be there when he needed it. The intangible assets were perhaps more apparent to me than to Charles, but were significant nonetheless. Charles himself constituted perhaps the greatest asset of all. His expertise and experience, combined with his creative and innovative intellect, made him an indispensible element of the plan's success. In addition, his company sat on a vast reservoir of goodwill from his customers and in the close relationships with the other independent retailers who would be selling his products.

You and your CP should imagine there are subfolders to fill for all the items in the required inventory for carrying out the plan. Lastly, bear in mind that even after you've identified all the necessary assets, you still have only half the information you need. You must also determine whether those assets will be available when you need them. You don't want to be waiting for the cavalry when the time for battle is now.

Question 5: What are the risks we will be facing?

In the first decades of the twenty-first century, business leaders have grown more openly skittish about random events that seem to cause havoc with their best-laid plans with increasing regularity. Dubbed "black swans" by the author and New York University professor Nassim Taleb, these sometimes catastrophic phenomena mock our attempts to assess future risk with any accuracy, to predict the inherently unpredictable. Despite our heightened awareness of catastrophic risk, however, I continue to spend quite a bit of time and energy listening for the comparatively more mundane risks to a plan. Rather than dwell on the macro-risks that often consume strategy and planning theorists, let me address some risks a bit closer to the action, which are more likely to impact most business plans. When it comes to discussions about risk, I can turn to the writings of my former McKinsey colleague Lowell Bryan. While acknowledging that the future is largely unforeseeable, and that all planning is precarious, Bryan came up with a practical framework for determining the levels of knowable risk around future initiatives, and building that knowledge into a workable plan of action. Simply put, Bryan suggested laying out the multiple initiatives that would allow an organization to proceed with its strategy while regularly reevaluating its commitment to any one initiative as it came closer to maturity. He illustrated the idea using a grid, with one axis representing risk, and the other representing the proposed time frame, on which he laid out the initiatives under way. This allowed for spot assessments of which initiatives were in the pipeline and the level of uncertainty or risk associated with each one. Later Bryan added the further dimension of the return anticipated from each initiative.

You can't ignore risks like political upheavals, technological game-changers, or natural disasters, but you can't do anything about those, either. Instead, you can focus your listening on the relevant, short-term identifiable risks over which you have some control. I keep some basic risk questions in the front of my mind. First, who will object to the plan? Objections could come from outside the organization—perhaps from customers, regulators, suppliers, or competitors. Or they might come from colleagues within the organization who see the initiatives you have in mind as threatening their success in some way. Either way, I like to ensure that my CP and I are going into a plan having tried to look at it through the eyes of every group that might be affected by it, and have discussed whether or not we can head off or lessen any objections.

The second question concerns what I call *first step risk*. "Getting off on the right foot" is a useful phrase to keep in mind for listening for and understanding risks. How many times have you planned something really well and find that phase one torpedoes the whole effort? Think back a generation to the Coca-Cola Company's infamous introduction of New Coke. The public's response was immediate and vicious, and the company returned to the original formula only three months later. As it has been reported, more careful listening might have helped them avert this disaster.

The third question is, "What are the major barriers down the road that can derail our journey toward success?" Your CP must consider all the possible trouble spots, plan how to mitigate those risks where possible, and agree to remind the two of you as time goes on to revisit your assessment of risk and reevaluate your plans for mitigation and avoidance.

Fourth, I like to ask the question: "Is there anything in this company's, or this industry's, history that we've overlooked that could point to trouble?" I'm often surprised to find that a similar plan was attempted in the past and faced a threat or challenge. Yet managers often fail to consider such past troubles when pursuing a similar plan. It's smart to remember the words of Harry Truman: "The only thing new in this world is the history you don't know."

I had no doubt that my friend Charles knew the risks involved in taking such a big step with his business, but I couldn't say for certain that he was taking them seriously enough. The rag trade wasn't the same as it had been when he was first starting out. Even at the upper end of the market, the old-line European designers and manufacturers were facing stiff competition, especially when it came to costs and pricing, from every corner of the globe, especially from Asia, where mills in places like China had access to inexpensive labor and materials, even if they still lacked some expertise. Charles certainly paid lip service to this threat, but seemed to be trying to brush it aside. I kept at him with a barrage of questions, until we were able to articulate the heart of the problem: he would be trying to carve out a niche for himself at the high end of the supply chain, which was coming under increasing pressure from lower-cost manufacturers. Together we recognized that a time was coming when even high-end suits would be tailored for much less than the cost at which Charles's factory could make them. Even with great styling and merchandising this would make the factory purchase a questionable deal.

Most important, the plan's greatest asset also constituted its greatest risk factor: Charles himself. What if he became ill, or for some other reason was unable to oversee the operation? Could the plan succeed in his absence? When we put this question on the table, Charles began to think more realistically about whether he was getting too far over his skis. He recalled that there were other examples of vertical integration in his industry that had failed because the managers had taken on too much. They had become distracted and began ignoring their core businesses. Charles and I batted these risks back and forth for quite some time. In truth, he was filled with excitement when we began to talk, but his enthusiasm became more measured as we brought some of these risks into focus. At the end of the day, Charles reluctantly concluded that the risks were too great to justify the investment, and he chose not to go forward with the deal.

• • •

I offer this as an example of productive give-and-take; a conversation between two people listening to each other carefully in an atmosphere of acceptance and respect that enabled us to remain calm and thoughtful, to keep our minds open and challenge assumptions, so that my friend could make an informed decision. I'm sure he was disappointed in the final result, but the fact that he made a difficult decision is a testament to his ability to get beyond his personal desires and do what was right for his company.

In addition to enabling you to determine whether your initiatives are keeping your company moving in the right direction, the information you accumulate in the folders in your Plan drawer can help you determine whether the return on those initiatives is going to be worth the investment risks. Some initiatives lend themselves to concrete and rigorous financial analyses that will give a quantitative answer to this question. In my view, those initiatives are the easier ones to assess. Other initiatives are less cut-and-dried, involving either less tangible assets or more subjective merits or opportunity costs that are difficult to define. These initiatives demand greater focus and diligence, and can crowd your bandwidth. In either case, your Plan folders supply the inputs you need to solve the critical return equation you'll use to judge the value of your plan and reshape it as necessary.

(((9)))

What Is the Team?

Many years ago, I met a merchant marine officer I'll call Popeye. A somewhat older man, he had spent his life as a sailor, and it showed: gruff and gravelly voiced, muscular and weather-beaten, he was the kind of man people describe as "an old salt." He enjoyed telling me his many tales of life at sea. As a shipboard officer, Popeye understood better than most the intricacies of getting a crew of sometimes difficult and stubborn seamen to work together efficiently, with minimal conflict. He believed, however, that sometimes it simply couldn't be done, that despite the presence of trusted old hands with great work records, at times the chemistry wasn't there, and the voyage was a misery for everyone. In those cases, he felt there was little benefit in trying to weed out the troublemakers or salvage some good people, and that the most efficient measure was to get rid of the whole crew and start fresh. Popeye told me that he used to send someone up to tie a broom to the highest smokestack on the ship as he sailed into port, as a signal to the company men in the harbor towers that he wanted a clean sweep of the crew. "Get rid of 'em all," he said, "and just start over."

In the world of business, as in Popeye's world, we typically need a crew to get anything done. Unlike in Popeye's world, we rarely have the opportunity to make a clean sweep, which is why I work hard to fine-tune my listening when it comes to matters of personnel and team. Never forget that a game plan is only as good as the players assigned to execute it. To me, a "team" is any group of people working together with a common purpose, whether it is assembled by design or comes together organically. The term doesn't have to denote a formal work team designed and assembled by management. Such teams exist—indeed, much has been written about them—but more often than not teams are informal and sometimes temporary groupings. You might find yourself part of a team of just two people, or you might work in a company that sees individual departments or divisions as teams. Even the hiring of a single individual for a job is an exercise in team-building.

It's frighteningly easy to make a bad call about people, and the results of a misstep here can be disastrous. I've also seen how the right shift in personnel, or a timely addition of a key individual, helps turn around a struggling organization. In fact, I once watched it play out both ways with the same position in the same company. I was consulting to the CEO of a large health-insurance company who needed to replace the chief operating officer he himself had brought in only a year and a half earlier.

The company had lost its previous COO at a time when its performance was slipping. Margins had shrunk and the resulting financial pressures had brought down the morale within the company, as well as its reputation. I didn't observe the first search process, but knowing that the CEO was a proven, seasoned executive, I'm sure he went about it thoughtfully. He chose a candidate from outside the company, a man I'll call Chandler, who was very much in the CEO's image: polished and patrician, with a pedigree that included all the right schools and all the right professional experience. In hindsight, it's reasonable to conclude that the CEO placed a high priority on his own comfort level with this key member of the management team. His hiring of Chandler—an executive so much like him—might also have reflected the CEO's conviction that he could have done the COO's job himself, had he enough hands. As it turned out, Chandler was simply the wrong man for the job. The company's performance continued to deteriorate, and the new COO was removed after only eighteen months. Not only was the expected turnaround nowhere in sight, but the company's reputation was further tarnished.

The CEO needed to bring in a new chief operating officer quickly. Not wanting to repeat the same mistake, the CEO sought my advice about finding a replacement. I began by asking him what had convinced him to hire Chandler in the first place. His simple answer said it all: "I fell in love," he said, meaning that Chandler had appealed to him on a gut level, leaving the CEO little room for disciplined business judgment. I recognized that without a systematic approach that identified a set of key factors for which we needed to listen, we would have only our intuition and instincts on which to base our decision. There was no reason to believe that our instincts had any more value than those of the CEO the first time around.

I set about sharing my file folders for the Team drawer with the CEO, ultimately focusing on a short list of critical questions that would inform the search and that would factor into the many discussions he would have throughout the process. I have adopted those questions as a foundation for any conversation concerning personnel. I've found them useful across a broad range of situations. You can turn to them if you are a manager charged with assembling a work team for a project or an assignment; if you are hiring to fill a key post or group of positions in your organization; if you are an entrepreneur seeking to add a business partner; when you are considering taking a job in a new company or joining a work group within your current one; and when you find yourself looking to improve a dysfunctional team of which you are already a part.

After the CEO had narrowed his search to two finalists, these questions allowed him to make a comprehensive assessment of each one before making a decision. Both men had spent a long time with the company. One candidate, Larry, had virtually grown up there, starting out in the mailroom and working his way up through all levels of the operation over a thirty-year career. Larry didn't come from the more cultivated world of Chandler and the CEO—his demeanor smacked more of the lunch pail than the boardroom—but his rough-hewn exterior masked an intellect that was both quick and deep. The other man, Russell, had been with the company only a few years less than Larry, most of which he spent in the executive ranks. On the outside, Russell cut a somewhat more polished figure, as if he were more naturally suited to stand at the right hand of the CEO, but Larry was as competent and determined as Russell. Neither candidate was the obvious first choice. They each had clear strengths and some potential weaknesses. I encouraged the CEO to use the following questions to focus his listening as he interviewed the two candidates and sought feedback about them from other members of his management team.

Question 1: What capabilities do we need?

I often find that people ask the wrong opening question when it comes to teams. They start by asking *who* they need on a team, when first they should be asking what the members of the team need to be able to do. If you're filming a movie, you know you need a camera operator, lighting people, sound technicians, electricians and construction people, prop masters and drivers. Depending on the size of the production, and the skills of the prospective team members, maybe some of those capabilities can be combined, but that's not your concern at this stage. First, you need to develop a comprehensive list of what the team must be able to accomplish.

In the case of our health-insurance company, Larry and Russell brought complementary capabilities to the table. Larry knew the operation from the ground up, and had a knack for getting things done. He was aggressive and demanding, and people seemed more than willing to follow his lead, respecting his experience and trusting his judgment. Larry was more than simply a man of the people, though. He had an incisive mind and an extraordinary command of the numbers. Russell had longer experience as a high-level executive, and a record of proven success. If Larry had the brashness of a drill sergeant, Russell had the quiet confidence of a seasoned officer, with an ability to build and lead productive work teams.

Question 2: What are the mind-sets of the team members?

This may sound a little vague, or difficult to get a handle on, but it is critical information that can be revealed through careful questioning. Does everybody under consideration for the team understand the organizational mandate, as well as the individual objective or initiative for which they are responsible? Do they all support it with a shared level of enthusiasm and urgency? Is there alignment? When seeking information for this folder, remember that any individual within an organization brings his or her own personal goals and aspirations to an enterprise. When putting together a team for a project or an initiative, you have to remain vigilant that not only do these individual mandates align with the company's mandate, but that the personal idiosyncratic mandates of each of the team members will mesh with those of their colleagues.

As the CEO listened to the two candidates and others in the company who had important perspectives, he discovered that there weren't many tangible differences between Russell and Larry concerning mind-sets. They shared a sense of enthusiasm about the tasks ahead of them, and neither were in any doubt about what needed to be done. There was, however, a quality of impatience about Larry that stood out. It seemed as though his only gear was overdrive, as if he had decided that there'd be plenty of time to sleep when he was dead, and he had little tolerance for those who didn't share his attitude. Larry loved to tell the story about his high school track coach, who would tell his 440-yard runners, "Run the first 220 yards as fast as you possibly can, and then in the second half, pick up the pace."

Question 3: What are the roles of the team members?

There are really two components to this question. First, this is where you compare the skill sets of the individual team members with the list of capabilities you've laid out. Can some team members serve multiple roles? Do some functions require more than one person? You want to make sure that every capability on your list is covered completely. Second, you have to remain mindful of group dynamics anytime you put people together and ask them to do anything as a team. Think about whether the team requires a leader, or can function as a group of equals. Are there natural leaders and followers on the team? Too many of each, too few, or the right proportions? Will the roles played generate unnecessary competitiveness or jockeying for position that could undermine the efforts of the team? Do you need to impose some kind of structure or hierarchy onto the planning of the team, or can you let it take shape organically?

Keep in mind that sometimes you can't be as cut-and-dried about defining roles within a team as you want to be. For instance, sometimes a team gets built around a single star performer, in the way a sports team builds around a "franchise player." Other times, people might find themselves assigned to a team because someone believed them to be great "natural athletes"—that is, smart, energetic people who have proved themselves to be fast learners, creative and resourceful—who would carve out a role for themselves as the team got down to work.

Returning to Larry and Russell, this question didn't advance either of the candidates ahead of the other, although the answers to this question revealed significant differences between them. Russell was the more complete executive, and assumed the mantle of authority more easily. For his part, Larry had great instincts, with more years in the trenches. You could picture him leading a charge with his sword held high. At the same time, you could see Russell winning battles and wars with strategy and cunning, brilliantly moving his armies around on the planning table, and picking the right field generals for each maneuver. A strong case could be made for either man taking a leadership role.

Question 4: Will this assignment be good for the individuals on the team?

Managers often get so absorbed in figuring out who might be good for a work team that they forget to question whether being on the team will be good for the people assigned to it. A team of people who feel both challenged and fulfilled are more likely to turn in a superior performance. There are so many possible permutations related to individual development: Does the team represent a chance for a person to develop leadership skills? Can it be a way to unite talented people who you need to work better together? Will more experienced team members take advantage of an opportunity to mentor younger workers? Does the project or initiative require some element of institutional memory, and can any of the team members provide it? Does the team's objective touch a nerve or flame the passions of the individuals? Can the assignment itself represent a reward of some kind?

Even Larry would have probably admitted that the position of chief operating officer represented a stretch for him, but also meant that the potential for growth was possibly larger. For Russell, it was the next logical step on his career path. The flip side of his natural trajectory is that he knew its growth slope and had a fairly good guess at where it would end up. Larry's future was less clear; this job could be the end of the line for him, or he might knock it out of the park and go on to even greater things. The CEO saw less risk in choosing Russell, but perhaps the chance of greater rewards from Larry.

Question 5: What are the inescapable realities?

For all the talk these days of "dream teams," managers and strategists don't usually have the luxury of choosing players from a limitless pool of talent. Sometimes, you have to do your best with the players you've got, and make sure you don't end up with a team that looks like the Bad News Bears, only without the positive result. The best people for a particular job might be needed elsewhere. Maybe you can't afford them, or maybe they're already working for the competition. Customer preferences, personal loyalties and countless other unpredictable and sometimes seemingly irrational factors can govern the composition of a team.

One inevitable reality is what I refer to as the "personnel tax." The simple fact is that not everybody is above average, nor should they be. True, General Electric's storied former leader, Jack Welch, used to believe that a company should clean out the bottom 10 percent of performers from its workforce, but that's not always the way things play out. Because many organizations believe in giving workers every extra chance to do their best work, or to reward enthusiastic effort and loyalty, or to maximize their positive impact on a community by maintaining high staffing levels, these organizations will inevitably include some journeymen. It is important to maximize every team member by doing the best you can to match their roles and responsibilities to their capabilities.

A manager's primary task is to listen well enough to discern the potential weaknesses and trouble spots of a team, and make every effort to fill and compensate. But secondly, managers can help foster a spirit of acceptance, support, and cooperation, to prevent resentments from eating away at a team from the inside, and to make it possible for it to perform to its greatest potential.

As is usually the case, neither of the two contenders for COO, Russell or Larry, was an obvious favorite, but they were the only two options within the company, and the board really didn't want the CEO to consider external candidates again. One unexpected reality—the kind of factor that is difficult to anticipate—weighed in favor of Russell. Because it seemed that his career had been aiming at this position for some time, he had come to feel it was his due, that it was his turn. Others within the company shared this opinion, including most of the members of the board of directors, who felt that

Russell had earned this opportunity. Many feared that he would leave the company if he did not get the job, which would mean losing a valuable member of the team.

In this case, the CEO had to restrict his choices to the people closest at hand. But such a restriction raises an important point. There are countless factors that can limit the options when building teams and finding good people—some of them traps of our own making. When I think about these realities, my mind always conjures up the image of Claude Rains as Captain Renault in the climactic scene of the film *Casablanca*. As Humphrey Bogart stuffs a still-smoking pistol into the pocket of his trench coat after shooting the enemy officer, Rains turns to his underlings and orders, "Round up the usual suspects." Time and time again, executives and managers reflexively turn to the familiar people at hand to carry out a plan, either because they fear upsetting an established way of working, or perhaps because it never occurs to them that other options exist. This phenomenon is as common as it is unwise, a vivid illustration of the status quo bias leading to fuzzy thinking. I've even seen managers turn away from a good plan because they can't think broadly enough to assemble a team that could accomplish it. If there are not realities limiting your choices, don't let yourself get trapped by your own habits. Challenge your assumptions about personnel and team as vigorously as you would in any other area.

Question 6: How is the chemistry?

It's no secret that a team full of superstars doesn't guarantee victory. How many sports teams have emptied their coffers and snatched up glamorous free agents, only to find that the locker room was too small to contain all those outsize personalities and egos? Personality is both subtle and protean, and even when you think you've got a person figured out, they show you that the only thing you can count on is inconsistency. When you start to combine people into work teams, to weave together contrasting threads of personality, you set up the potential for conflicts too numerous to count, but at the same time, you never know when a group of people will come together to create a spark of magic.

I've found, over the years, that all teams have some level of tolerance for misfits. It may be that an individual brings a high enough level of talent or a unique skill set to a team that outweighs his or her difficult behavior. Or, conversely, a less-skilled worker may bring some intangible quality—humor, generosity, enthusiasm—that makes him valuable to a team.

The chemistry question would also likely come down in favor of Russell, who was smoother, and a more recognizable commodity with a more familiar style in the eyes of his peers on the executive floor. No doubt, Larry was the spikier personality. He created more friction when he rubbed up against people, but he also generated more passion. Larry was magnetic, and it was easy to believe that people would go to war with him if he asked.

Question 7: What are the consequences of performance?

Finally, I return to our principle of alignment. Starting with mandate and expanding downward through objectives and initiatives and personal aspirations, a shared understanding of a clearly articulated purpose is the foundation of success. The same principles apply to teams: every individual working in a group must share an understanding of what success will look like. Individuals on the team, and the team collectively, must define and agree to the goals, incentives, and the consequences of failure. Getting teams to work well together is enough of a challenge under the best of circumstances. Imagine the potential chaos if people are working with different expectations about success or failure.

On the face of it, there was no discernible difference between Larry and Russell when the CEO contemplated the consequences of their performance. You could certainly say that Larry had a great deal more to prove, to the board and the CEO, and possibly to himself, than Russell did, but it was clear that failure in the position would have been equally devastating to both of them.

• • •

People come into business situations with résumés and pedigrees and objective measures of experience and prior success, but matters of character, suitability, and interpersonal chemistry are difficult to quantify. Instinct and intuition, while undeniably relevant when it comes to assembling good teams or fixing dysfunctional ones, can only take you so far, so I find it comforting to know that I have a listening process in place that can help me challenge or confirm my gut feelings.

The health-insurance CEO embraced this approach as he made the personnel decision. He sourced information and ideas about the two candidates from across his management team and his board of directors, ensuring that he had a deep reserve of data in each of his file drawers that could inform his decision. As he conversed with each of these individuals, including the two candidates, he exhibited truly exceptional listening skills, staying actively engaged through deliberate questioning and probing. At the end of this process, I think he was surprised by the decision he came to: the position of chief operating officer went to Larry. The CEO later told me that as he listened to Larry's gritty and no-nonsense presentation of his thoughts about what he could do in the position, the CEO detected a deep level of commitment. He also heard a consistent refrain from his most trusted colleagues that Larry's style and managerial approach were quite different from his own. From that feedback the CEO deduced that their complementary styles could deepen and expand the company's management capabilities. Larry's commitment and his singular style proved to be the winning edge; eighteen months into his tenure, the company had reestablished its forward momentum, and was looking toward the future with optimism.

Larry had not merely risen to the challenge; he had fully integrated himself into the leadership of the company. What Larry revealed about himself was that for all his bluster, he was actually an extremely good listener. What I observed was that Larry spent an enormous amount of time with his various teams, gathering the facts he needed to make informed and rational decisions. Larry's continued success demonstrated the one remaining truism concerning teams: You can never stop listening, whether you're actually on the team, or otherwise responsible for the creation and performance of the team. The information gathered in these file folders is necessary not just at the time of formation of a team or a workforce, but at every stage of its existence. Larry never forgot that people and personalities change and grow and mutate over time. He understood that the information he was working with had a limited shelf life. You must always have an ear to the ground; you must always be listening and refreshing the information in your folders, giving the people in the company the best opportunity to make the good decisions and commit to the right actions to increase your business's chance of success.

(((10)))

How Will We Get It Done?

A promising team is assembled around a clearly articulated and enthusiastically supported mandate and has set all the pieces of a detailed and comprehensive plan into motion. The whole operation is pointed toward true north, and then, the whole thing goes south. Why couldn't an initiative that had been carefully thought through get carried out successfully? What went wrong with the execution? These vexing questions are perhaps the most common in our daily business lives. Nothing will push you to distraction like the botched play.

In the course of my business career, I've learned that there are a few critical elements that are essential to successful execution. When I listen to people talk about the operational challenges they're anticipating, I almost always hear some reference to one of these elements. These are the topics I listen for, and that guide the questions I ask when I deal with executional issues. The labels on the file folders in my Execution drawer—*decision-making, information, complexity,* and *rhythm*—may be rather broad, but this is by design. Problems related to unanticipated complexity or a poorly defined chain of responsibility, for example, will arise at any level of an organization, whether you're a pizza-delivery driver coordinating with the kitchen staff of your store, the regional manager of that pizza chain managing inventory and supply levels, or a chef in the national headquarters trying to determine standard cooking times for the new special extra-large pie offered at the holidays. Each of these questions applies to one-on-one interactions at most levels in an organization, and so can have as much relevance to an executive responsible for implementing the corporate strategic plan as to the warehouse manager getting the trucks loaded on time.

Question 1: How are we making decisions?

The typical catechism regarding decisions addresses *who* is making *what* decisions, and *when*, which of course are the fundamental questions. In my experience, I've found that most managers listen fairly well for evidence that these elements are fully understood and effective. But there are two more challenging decision-making questions that force managers to raise their listening game. First, can an organization identify and correct faulty decision making? And second, how does the organization allow for managers to go outside the decision-making routine when necessary?

Imagine that you've been tasked with opening a fast-food chain in China, with a projected one hundred stores up and running within three years. How many decisions do you think the people in your organization will have to make daily to keep that effort moving forward? The number could probably be over a thousand in the first week. With so many decisions needing to be made, mistakes will inevitably happen, and when they do you must be able to listen so you can identify and correct bad or late decisions along the way. If you aren't prepared to correct for missteps in executing a plan, you are in big trouble before you begin.

Early in my career, I learned an important lesson about how to listen in order to correct faulty decision-making processes. At UCLA, where I did my surgical residency, we met on Saturday mornings for "Mortality and Morbidity" conferences, at which the senior surgical residents would present cases with poor outcomes for review by the faculty. If there were a lot of cases to discuss, the conference might drag into the afternoon, which added to the woes of the residents, since Saturday afternoon was our only time off. The first time I attended one of these conferences, I was struck by how brutally the faculty dissected and challenged the decision making of the residents, and how determined the instructors were to single out a resident to point a finger at, even when it seemed clear that no error had been found. I asked one of the senior surgeons why it was assumed that someone had erred. Wasn't it possible that a patient had a complicated course, or worse had died, because of the nature of the disease or injury, or the idiosyncratic path the case had taken? The surgeon looked at me sternly and replied, "We can't correct blameless errors, so we assume there aren't any."

If an error in judgment could be identified, the faculty could create a teaching opportunity around it. It was no fun to be at the center of one of those teaching moments, but we all survived them. To be sure, none of us residents ever forgot those lessons in sound medical practice. The transferable point is simple: If you can't identify a decision maker, or group of decision makers, and the mistake that has been made, you will have a tough time improving any initiative under way. This is not about blame, but about responsibility. Ducking responsibility is counterproductive, and impedes progress. People who hide in the shadows when problems arise are the company's assassins. Accountability is not about punishment; it's about identifying weaknesses in process or gaps in information that can be repaired or filled. It's about constant improvement. Mistakes are inevitable, but they don't have to be repeated. People who own their mistakes are precious, because for these people, growth and improvement are possible.

Listening for how decisions are made and ensuring that everyone involved understands the chain of command and who has what kind of authority, will of course increase any organization's odds of smooth and successful execution of its plan. Once that basic operating structure is in place, it will serve the company well, as long as all the elements on which it is predicated go as expected—which, as we all know, occurs a lot less often than we'd like. This leads us to the second challenging decision-making question: What happens when unexpected stuff threatens to take us off course? Perhaps it sounds a little counterintuitive, but there must be clearly articulated procedures at the outset, so that people on the team can know what to do when seismic events shake the best-laid plans. If they have to take action that goes outside usual procedure, how will those actions be monitored? You must listen for whether everyone involved knows when such violations of the usual decision-making hierarchy are acceptable, and feels empowered to act unilaterally when necessary.

How can you tell if this willingness to improvise exists? A good technique is to listen for whether the team is asking about hypothetical scenarios. "What if we have to reduce price to make the deal? What if we have to expand our warranty terms? Can we just go ahead and do that?" Put another way, always listen for how a company's front line will know when to call an audible and when it's better to ask for forgiveness rather than permission.

Question 2: Are we getting the right information at the right time?

A sign on the wall of a university science lab reads, "If it can't be measured, it doesn't exist." I'm sure the folks in the philosophy department would take issue with that assertion, but it provides an important listening filter for conversations about execution. The decisions that originally set your plan in place all derive from a set of reliable information, and as you execute, an ongoing flow of new information will enable the inevitable course corrections. If you want to be able to execute successfully you need to be constantly listening for the source of the information, its reliability, and its timeliness. Metrics and milestones are your GPS when you put a set of initiatives into action, and information is what powers that GPS. Without good information, you cannot track and measure where you've been, where you are at any given moment, and where you're heading. A steady flow of information is also analogous to a weather report—how changing conditions affect your initiatives, and the impact of those initiatives on the customers, competitors, suppliers, and all the other stakeholders and conditions across the landscape.

With so many people fretting about information overload, perhaps there's something ironic about highlighting "Information" as a heading on a folder in my execution file drawer. That's actually the point: In an environment where a couple of keystrokes can produce a flood of data at any time, managers can be stymied by too much information as easily as by too little. If good execution depends on good information, it is incumbent on managers to ensure the integrity of the information on which they base their decisions. They need to qualify the sources. Just as important, they need to determine what data are relevant and important to their ongoing assessments, and what merely constitutes noise. And once the critical pieces of information have been identified, the next step is to know how often that information needs to be refreshed and reevaluated. If you stop and look too often, paralysis by analysis might set in. But a failure to look often enough could leave you in the dark. I know I've listened well and asked the right questions if I can picture the dashboard that will be in front of those responsible for executing a set of initiatives, and if I feel confident that the information will help keep the operation running smoothly.

Question 3: How do we manage complexity?

Albert Einstein spent a lifetime trying to make sense of a vast and incomprehensibly complex universe. Even Einstein knew that he had to somehow reduce the complexity of his subject just to be able to study it. "It can scarcely be denied," he said, "that the supreme goal of all theory is to make the irreducible elements as simple and as few as possible." That dictum has been repeated often, usually paraphrased as, "Everything should be made as simple as possible, but not simplistic." The theory of relativity is hardly simple. Processes and explanations always get down to a certain level of irreducibility at which, one hopes, they become manageable. Although Einstein was referring to complex scientific theories and mathematical expressions, he could have made that comment just as accurately about business tasks. Executing any plan will require you to manage through some level of complexity.

Businesses today operate within a much more complicated and rapidly changing environment than they did even five years ago. Just consider the increase in rules and regulations that apply to businesses, or how the Internet has affected the speed at which events impact our daily lives. I sometimes think that operating in such an environment is like trying to perform a violin concerto from the back of a bucking bronco. The complexity of the task itself is compounded by the context in which you are carrying it out. A good leader assumes the job of defining the complexity of an operation. He makes sure the team understands what it is they need to be concerned about and what they can ignore. For example, if a competitor's unexpected price reduction suddenly has a team questioning its retail strategy, it's up to the leader to tell the team whether to look the other way, to hold its pricing and stick to the plan. By carefully listening to his or her team, a manager can identify the developments and conditions that are outside the field of play, and then define the boundaries, thus reducing complexity. One executive, whom I very much admired, said it best: "My job is to do as much of the worrying around here as possible so everyone else can do their jobs."

Question 4: Do we have a rhythm?

The constant companion of complexity is chaos. Those managers who organize their conversations avoid chaos. When interactions take place on an overly *ad hoc* basis—when an organization has adopted a reactive stance, spending too much time chasing decisions about unfolding events and putting out fires—I consider that organization to be lacking in an essential ingredient to good execution: a managerial rhythm. The difference between a company with an established interaction and routine and one with meetings driven by random external factors is akin to the difference between a sober person trying to walk a straight line and someone who has been overserved.

Steady managerial rhythms provide the discipline that allows a company to stay out in front of changing conditions and to stay on task in the face of the inevitable barrage of unforeseen events.

Managerial rhythm to me means a time-regular set of interactions; be they one-on-one discussions or larger meetings, managers must commit to maintaining a communications calendar. Every individual on a work group or team should know what kind of interactions to expect and how often they will take place. A predetermined agenda will dictate which functions and capabilities need to be represented in those gatherings. Those attending should know what is expected of them going into the meeting, and the types of decisions and instructions they can expect to take away from this encounter. Lastly, everyone should expect that they may have to discuss the unexpected in these gatherings. The agenda must allow for a discussion of both fixed and variable factors—the questions and decisions addressed each time, and the irregular, unpredicted ones that can be just as important. With regular and ongoing interactions you establish a discipline in a company that ensures the gathering of focused and timely information and allows for precise measurements and calm decision making.

I've never seen a company as good at executing strategies as one of my most recent clients. No other organization comes close. Their corporate culture embraces excellence, and while the executive talent is truly exceptional, it is not the only secret sauce in their recipe. The magic ingredient, surprisingly, is its calendar. The CEO of this multinational circulates his operational calendar in December, with every operating review and upper-management meeting for the following year clearly laid out. Of course, the schedule may get tweaked as the year progresses, but there are few if any cancellations, and meetings are rarely rescheduled more than once. Every top manager in the company has a calendar that derives in major part from the

CEO's calendar, and this coordinated interaction cascades through the company. The various business units prepare for the meetings their senior leaders have with the boss, and as you might imagine, things tend to get done on time. Even with the daily events that cause breaks or syncopations in the managerial rhythms of the company, you can still sense a metronome beating in the hallways and dictating the regular interactions throughout its worldwide operations.

• • •

The questions on the four folders in my Execution drawer are highly interconnected. They overlap with, and in fact depend on, each other. By addressing one of them, you tend to address, at least to some degree, each of the others. Orderly decision making, access to timely and reliable information, thoughtful simplification, and predictable managerial rhythms add up to discipline and control in execution and also prepare the organization for some broken-field running when conditions change suddenly. When a leader listens carefully to sort through the execution challenges the result is much like a well-executed dive: everything where it should be, a smooth entry, and a high score for technique and grace. I'll share with you an example of one such effort to which I would give a top score.

I worked with a CEO just as he was taking over the leadership of a large financial company. The company was not in any obvious trouble at the time. A strong management team was in place, and on paper at least, business was good. This CEO, however, had the good sense to understand that it was not a time for complacency. He knew that the lack of immediate emergency gave him time to probe, to ask questions of the operation that might reveal whether the company was prepared to cope with shifting conditions. He told me how during his first months on the job he went on a virtual listening tour of his company, asking his managers about their operating routines. In the back of his mind was the question: Was the company comfortably sitting back on its heels or was it on its toes, leaning forward, ready to dart quickly in any direction should circumstances change?

The CEO's first clue that there was room for improvement surfaced when he realized that information and assessments were landing on his desk too late for him to effectively monitor the company's progress. Further, that information was arriving in an unfiltered bundle, making it too difficult to sort out the data that would serve as the company's metrics and connect to the business decisions needed to steer the operation.

On the plus side, everyone on his team had easy access to this information, but there were two factors that created a downside. One, there was no shared understanding of the context in which to interpret the data. Two, because no clear decision-making structure had been imposed, each and every member of the team felt empowered to draw conclusions from the data and to act on those conclusions. Decisions were being made—often, very good decisions—but neither the CEO nor anyone else on the management team could trace how some of those decisions came about. What would happen, he asked, in the case of a bad decision? He didn't care about finding a scapegoat, but rather understood the lesson I had learned in the Mortality and Morbidity conferences I attended as a surgical resident: blameless errors can't be corrected, and thus, will surely be repeated.

The CEO instituted a set of procedures that had a dramatic effect on the company. First, he created what he called a war room, a sort of command center at the company's headquarters where massive amounts of data were collected, tracked, and processed. The war room would pull together all the unfiltered data and sort through them to tease out the most useful pieces. These would then be organized into a weekly bulletin or dashboard update that would be disseminated to all the company's top leaders. The war room was also charged with tracking the company's progress on certain tasks and initiatives. It would identify the right metrics to follow and then produce regular updates that could be sent off to the various teams responsible for each plan.

Next, the CEO scheduled a weekly meeting, a global conference call at 8 A.M. every Monday that included managers from every corner of this vast operation. The dashboard updates produced by the war room would be sent out to each member of the team every Sunday, so they could prepare for the meeting. The call always occured, short a natural disaster, and every participant knew the agenda—what questions would be asked, what decisions would be made, and who would make them. Over time, as the team grew comfortable with the new rhythm of interaction, additional details were put into place. The team began assessing the data with a set of predetermined trigger points in mind, so that the numbers could point to certain actions when they reached certain levels.

These changes made a tremendous difference. What made it work was the specificity and predictability of it all. By organizing the decision-making process and reducing the pool of important information, the CEO found a way to cut through the complexity that would have impeded the company's execution. He was able to increase orderliness and discipline, which in turn increased both the steadiness of the operation and the likelihood of continued good fortune.

Even after you've honed and streamlined a plan and assembled a crack team, any venture can falter when you take it from the drawing board to the real world. We operate in a complex and volatile environment, in which conditions are both fluid and unpredictable, and success requires us to be constantly alert and flexible. In other words, we had better be good listeners if we are to navigate these often treacherous business seas, which is why it is so important to listen with vigilance for signs that execution processes are keeping the enterprise on course.

Is It Getting Personal?

At this point, you might be saying to yourself that the structured listening techniques I describe may work in a world populated by robots and automatons, but the real world is teeming with real people with all their quirks and impulses, hidden agendas and idiosyncratic values. I wouldn't blame you, and in fact that's why I have a separate file drawer marked "Personal." I've talked about the importance of decoupling from our emotions in order to become better listeners and communicators, and I've acknowledged that every discussion, whether it's about mandate or team building or managerial rhythms, is as original and unique as the individual people involved. Still, it would be understandable if you visualized the ideal listener I have described as a pointy-eared, hyperlogical Mr. Spock who grudgingly makes allowances for a world full of volatile Captain Kirks.

I should perhaps point out that a select few of the best business listeners I've encountered are sometimes near that description: the masters of methodical analysis and reason and emotionally neutral decision makers who tend to populate the elite executive chambers. This is not to say that they are cold-blooded and uncaring or that they are insensitive to the human dimension of the world in which they operate, or that they themselves are incapable of emotional connections. Like Spock, these executives are generally benevolent, but they accept that their position demands unyielding focus on information. Some of them would say that their job as a leader requires them to remain detached enough so that they can recognize and understand how the ideas and observations of the people in the ranks beneath them are influenced by emotion. Indeed, the best of them often suppress their own reflexive behaviors in order to listen better to the people around them, to discover what makes those people tick and how their human nature affects communication in a business setting. It may not win these executives a lot of close friends, but the role they play generates vast wellsprings of respect.

Most people will say that the companies they work in more closely resemble *The Office*, the television workplace comedy in which even the most mundane conversations are driven by all varieties of human foibles and vanities. The reality of business life is that in all our communications, we share some aspect of ourselves. Everything we communicate reveals something about who we are, how we think, what we feel, and what we think is important.

The hard information I glean from a business conversation exists in black and white. Facts are facts, and numbers are numbers. The character and mood of my conversation partner make up the palette that colors and shades the information. Most often, it is not a palette of bold primary colors, but rather a broad spectrum of subtle secondary colors—complex combinations that add nuance and depth to my understanding. And, sometimes, even some mystery. The occasional brilliant flashes of color equate, in my mind, to transient moods and emotional flare-ups, caused by inevitable life events and crises: a thrilling new romance or a devastating divorce, a health problem or a death in the family, troubled children or financial pressures. The impact of these events is real and profound, but rarely is it permanent. I see these moods in terms of strong colors because they are usually out there in plain sight, demanding attention. In some environments, your CP might even announce it at the beginning of a conversation. "I'm sorry I'm in a foul mood. I was up all night, worried sick about how my kid is doing in school, and I'm frustrated and exhausted." While they may color a person's experience of the world for the time being, they do not define that person's character.

Much more intriguing to me, and relevant to good listening, is an individual's intrinsic personality, analogous to the more subtle secondary colors that decorate their lives. Is he an optimist or pessimist? Is she cautious or impetuous? Coolly detached or emotionally invested in every action? Selfless or narcissistic? These characteristics do not wax and wane with passing moods; they define a person's very nature.

Let me offer a pair of anecdotes that illustrate how you can improve your listening by focusing attention on matters of personality. John had outlined an impressive promotional idea involving an end-of-aisle merchandising display. When I asked how the retailers had reacted to the idea, John's response was vague, though generally positive. He made an offhand remark that the retailers had commented about the size of the display, but assured us it was nothing important. With any of the other marketing people, I would have left it at that, but I knew I had to adjust my listening with John. He was an upbeat, very positive guy who always managed to get things done, and I liked him quite a bit. His glass wasn't merely half full, it was usually overflowing, which endeared John to everyone around him, and also made him a valuable team member. I had learned, however, that because of his innate positivity, John had a tendency to downplay anything potentially negative that he might hear. It was almost as if he became deaf to bad news. In this instance, we probed a bit deeper into what the retailers had said, and it became obvious that we needed to tweak those displays to make them fit. John needed his colleagues to augment his own listening and point out when this wonderful asset of his got in the way.

On the other side of the equation was Rosa, who took pride in her ability to see all sides of any issue. She was a meticulous analytical thinker and an adept problem solver. In contrast to John, Rosa's glass was always half-empty at best, a quality that she credited for her clarity of mind. We might have seen her as a dyed-in-the-wool pessimist, but she considered herself a realist, and believed that her ability to explore the downside of an issue, when others around her focused on the upside, enabled all kinds of valuable contingency planning. It was simply her nature, but I learned to filter my conversations with her so that I could listen through the fog of doubt that generally hung over them. Specifically, Rosa had a tendency to signal her negativity by pointing out a past error someone had made in similar circumstances. That kind of historical reference became a listening trigger for me, and would always cause me to hold off on any decisions or conclusions with Rosa, give the matter a chance to percolate, and then revisit it in a later conversation. Mind you, this is not to say that I didn't trust Rosa's judgment. Often enough, she would abandon her skepticism after some further thought, but if I found that she had not changed her view by the time we reopened the discussion, I knew I needed to listen well. Rosa was generally spot-on in her reassessments.

When I open the Personal file drawer, I'm listening for what makes a person click, for any factor—values, goals, biases, worries, blind spots, or conflicts—that might make me want to alter the conclusions I draw from the information in all the other file drawers. It's not possible to open a file folder for every character trait that a person might display. Instead, I've developed a series of questions that enable me to tease out practical and useful information about the ways in which a person's character might govern their behavior and color their communication. These questions differ from those in the other drawers in one fundamental way: they are not questions I ask of my CP, but they are questions I ask of myself. They force me to focus on what I need to know about people as human beings, as opposed to how they might fit into some organizational apparatus. If I'm not making my best effort to listen, I have to be prepared for mistakes in my decision making.

Question 1: What does this person value?

In 1950, the Japanese film director Akira Kurosawa burst onto the world cultural scene with his now classic film, *Rashomon*. The film, which won the Academy Award for Best Foreign Language Film, tells the story of a fateful encounter between a traveling samurai, his wife, and a highwayman four times—once each through the eyes of the three principal characters, and once by the only actual witness, albeit an unreliable one. Not surprisingly, while the narratives all describe the same event, culminating in the death of the samurai, the accounts differ wildly, and often contradict each other outright. Characters exaggerate their own roles in the drama, or project motivations onto the others. They see events through the filter of their own egos and their own deepest emotions. Each character's story emphasizes what is most important to that character. The film has entered the collective consciousness to such a degree that the subjectivity of perception is now often referred to as the *Rashomon* effect.

In ways far less dramatic than the motivations depicted in

Kurosawa's film, the core values and beliefs of a person can come into play in the context of business discussions. For instance, some people commit themselves to peak personal performance, while others make the group ethos their primary concern. I've known managers whose self-esteem very much depends on their orderliness and tidy efficiency, and others who take pride in their reputation as high-performing rule breakers. These values may have a moral dimension and for some people may cross over to a higher spiritual belief system. No doubt, there are as many examples and permutations as there are people. The simple point is that understanding the values at the core of your CP's nature will help you listen more accurately to the essence of their conversation.

Have you ever asked someone to execute a task and either gotten a flat-out "no" or found out in an ensuing conversation that this person wasn't ready to perform? I'm not referring to a case of sloth or disruptive behavior in a colleague, but a situation in which someone is experiencing a conflict between their closely held beliefs or their very self-image and the task at hand. Let me tell you about Steve, one of the most likable men I've come across in business, and one of the most honest. Steve valued good fellowship and generosity of spirit among coworkers as deeply as he valued candor and leadership backbone. We were working on an organizational change in his business that appeared to require the immediate removal of an underperforming manager. After many discussions, I believed that we were getting closer to a plan of action. However, despite my conscious efforts to listen closely, I hadn't picked up that Steve was experiencing an inner crisis. His honesty was colliding headlong with his basic kindness. The fact was that Steve believed the manager deserved another chance.

Steve placed a high value on personal loyalty, and on the possibility of redemption. He didn't give up on people easily. Steve's fundamental faith in people was a large part of what others found so appealing in him. Steve's honesty made him want to tell me his view. But another characteristic that made him so likable stopped him: he didn't want to tell me that he didn't agree with me. It's not that Steve was a weak executive, but he was careful, and slow to confront. He did make the personnel move, but not until almost a year later.

I don't doubt that I was right that the manager needed to go, but I also acknowledge that Steve may have been more right. After that year, everyone in the company knew that the manager had been given every chance, and had been treated fairly. The positive effect that had on the company may very well have been worth an additional year of lackluster performance.

How did I improve my subsequent interactions with Steve? To begin with, I developed a new understanding of the conflicts within him between his sense of fairness and loyalty to his people on the one hand, and the pressure of communicating difficult business decisions on the other. From that moment on, if I saw that Steve was agreeing with me, and recognized the goodwill for him that it triggered in me, I would stop the discussion cold and ask, "Steve, please be honest with me. Am I hearing that you are agreeing, and that you will take action now?" He was too honest a man to give me anything less than a straight answer to that question.

Another very common way in which people express their personal value system is through their definition of success. Let's say a project team or a department has been productive and profitable, but the people in that group were at each other's throats the entire time, and the road to success was littered with hard feelings and bruised egos. A manager who values a harmonious workplace and a corporate culture that emphasizes employee growth and development might have reported the experience as a disheartening failure, or at least described the team as requiring corrective action. A different kind of manager, one who values bottom-line results, might not have cared at all about the tensions and conflicts on the team, or might not even have noticed. His report would boast of positive results, and say nothing about process.

If I'm sitting across the table from either of these managers, intending to make use of their assessment of the group's performance into our ongoing plans, I have to be acutely aware of the ways in which my CP's personal priorities and values are shaping the perceptions he or she is sharing. Otherwise, I have no hope of making any properly informed decisions.

Question 2: What are the individual's personal aspirations?

This is, in many ways, closely connected to the values question, but I call it out separately for a reason. In my career, both as a manager of people and as a consultant, I have often been surprised by how greatly people's perception of their own potential can differ from my assessment of it. I'm not talking about people with an overblown self-image, although that's certainly common enough. What never ceases to amaze me is that so many people err in the opposite direction, by undervaluing their own potential, when others around them see greater possibilities for them than they can imagine for themselves.

How do conflicting perceptions of potential affect communication? It goes back to the bedrock principle of challenging all assumptions. I confess that more than once, I've found myself laying out plans and ideas for a company that were based on my assumptions of where a particular individual would be, professionally, within a certain amount of time. Later, however, I would realize that the person was dumbfounded by what I had envisioned for him or her. If people don't share a fundamental understanding of what they can and cannot achieve, their communication will inevitably be at cross-purposes. It's very hard to have high aspirations for your organization if you have low aspirations for yourself.

A misalignment regarding aspirations can play itself out in a very different way. Let's imagine a particularly ambitious executive who wants nothing more than for his or her division to be the best in the company, possibly the best in the industry. This person wants to be known as a force to be reckoned with. At first glance, you might think that there's no way this ambition could be bad, but what if the executive's relentless drive is diverting resources that the company needs elsewhere in order to fulfill its overall strategy? It may be that your CP has as much confidence in his aspirations as you do, but has a different timetable. He might see himself on the fast track, when the organization needs him in place to see a long-term project through to completion.

The more you are attuned to an individual's personal aspirations—and the more sensitive you can be to the many ways in which they might run counter to the organization's plans for that person, or to the short-term needs of the organization, or possibly even to the overall mandate—the more effectively you'll be able to filter your listening.

Question 3: How does this person interact with colleagues and others?

We have all had to work with difficult people. As tough as it is to work side by side with an abrasive personality, it's an even greater challenge to manage one. Sure, sometimes a person is simply more trouble than he or she is worth, but those are the easy cases: those people are usually gone soon enough. I'm talking about the ones who make the lives of others less than pleasant, maybe even miserable, but at the same time make a measurable contribution to the organization. These are the people who can make your life difficult. They require patience and finesse, and often a lot of tolerance. Remember that when we were filling the file folders in our Team drawer, a degree of tolerance was highly desirable. Difficult people are part of the reason for that.

Conversations with problematic personalities demand that you filter your listening in an unusual manner. As soon as you realize that there are issues of character or personal style with your CP that either could raise your hackles so that you'll miss important information, or cause your CP to twist or distort the information being conveyed, you have to be on guard. Every conversation has value, and you need to make the decision to listen past the unpleasantness so you can stay tuned in for the nuggets of gold that earned your CP a place at the table to begin with.

Likability can throw communications off track as easily as unpleasantness can. Have you ever come away from a conversation scratching your head and wondering how you let yourself get talked into something? It's human nature to have a higher level of trust and confidence in someone about whom you have positive feelings. And it's easy to see how that might cause you to loosen your listening discipline.

I suggest that you rate your emotional response to your CPs on a kind of mental scale. Most people fall into the big middle, as on a bell curve, but it's the handful of people at either of the ends who will cause you problems. At one end are the true good guys who instantly engender trust and goodwill. With someone like this, you have to be conscious of how vulnerable you can be to their siren call, and constantly remind yourself to probe as deeply and carefully as you would in any other conversation. At the other end of the spectrum are the people who simply make you uncomfortable, whether or not they've actually done anything wrong. When you find yourself in conversation with someone you consider an unpleasant character, you may find it nearly impossible to cut them any slack. But if you don't, you're almost certain to miss something important.

Question 4: What is the person's level of self-awareness?

This is not always an easy question to answer. What I'm looking for here is a clue to my CP's level of emotional maturity. Are they reflective and good at self-diagnosis? Are they willing and able to see themselves as others see them? How well do they understand their own biases and predilections? So many popular psychology books are devoted to "getting in touch with our feelings," or our inner something-or-other, or to assessing our emotional intelligence, that we may be slightly dismissive of the question, but it's not to be taken lightly. By determining your CP's level of self-awareness, you can understand how he may or may not be consciously filtering what he says to you. It can be a listening challenge, a little like having to listen through multiple layers of studio enhancement so that you can hear someone's true voice on a recording.

For example, I've found that it pays to listen closely for one key aspect of personality: a person's relationship with *risk*. Some of us are more willing to roll the dice than others. Some people see trouble lurking around every corner and so are reluctant to venture into the unknown. Some will go to any lengths to protect their status and position. None of this is what primarily concerns me here, since it's a given that everyone has his own unique comfort level with risk. What

I want to know is whether or not my CP is self-aware enough so that he can understand but then separate his emotional relationship with risk from the practical assessments of threats and opportunities in the business environment. This is my central point: someone with a highly developed sense of self is going to be a valuable CP; he will make your listening job easier by signaling in advance what filters you'll need to have in place to strip out the noise that distorts his own communication.

• • •

In assembling this book, I wrestled with how to address this all-important file drawer of Personal issues. The questions in other chapters are aimed at gathering content, but this chapter's questions explore the quality of that content. While it would be nice to think that listening and communication break down into a set of purely objective factors, the fact is that the question of who we are as people pervades everything we do. We all want to think objectively about the widgets we have to make, but we can't lose sight of the fact that those widgets are made by human beings, for other human beings. It's why we do what we do.

SECTION

THREE

Reaping the Benefits

Now that we've taken this simple, everyday activity of listening and broken it down and picked it apart in ways you perhaps never thought possible, it's time to put it back together again, and return to our original question: How can we improve our judgment and decision making, our performance, and ultimately, the quality of our work experience, through better listening habits?

As is usually the case, it's best to clean your own house first, before you set out to help remake an organization or company so that it can reap all the benefits of good listening. Make sure your own listening practices are where you want them to be. With that idea in mind, I've divided this concluding section into two parts. To begin, we'll look at how listening informs good judgment, enabling a series of definable processes that I believe will lead you to better decisions, more often. The higher one travels up the ladder of management, the more substantial the challenges seem to be. Most likely, you'll be confronting at least one large-scale material question at any given time: Should we add to our product mix? Can we compete in new markets?

Is it time to update our corporate image? Can we get more productivity out of our factories? You will also address questions of a more tactical nature that entail filtering multiple inputs and generating positive action. Regardless of the issue on the table, the individuals with well-honed listening reflexes are going to cut through the noise and distractions and make the right moves most often and most efficiently.

Next, we can expand the discussion and explore some ways to build those processes, and all the habits of good listening on which they depend, into the routine of your organization. You can recognize a company that has organized itself around good listening and effective communications. There seems to be, perhaps paradoxically, no wasted breath, but at the same time, nothing is kept under wraps or left unsaid. There are rhythms and routines in the organization that demand discussion of all questions in such a way as to ensure transparency and put all assumptions on the table. Even when decisions involve a degree of uncertainty and risk, they can be made with confidence and "all deliberate speed."

If you've conjured up an image of a well-oiled machine in your mind, you're right, but only half right. As smooth and successful as an operation may be, it is still a human endeavor, the product of people working together with a common purpose. Efficiency doesn't necessarily translate into a robotic or antiseptic workplace. On the contrary, peak performance is a reward in itself for many of us. I think of the film *Apollo 13* and that team of engineers and technicians working feverishly, but with the utmost care, to piece together the equipment that would bring those astronauts home. I think of those smaller colleges who send basketball teams to the NCAA Final Four because those teams seem to always find a way to transcend expectations and raise their game to a magical plane. I go back to that endless weekend of surgeries in Watts so many years ago, and still feel a sense of pride and accomplishment remembering the pulsing rhythm of the OR as the team snapped into action each time they wheeled in a new patient.

Whatever your profession or your position, there's no greater thrill than to be in that groove, to enter the "zone," when time seems to slow down, and everything falls into place. Rarely does that experience lead to failure. It's that quality of performance that all organizations and leaders aspire to, and I believe it starts with establishing the best listening habits in every corner of an organization.

Connecting Better

Listening to Better *Judgment*

There is no blueprint for improving how you think, how you make better judgments, and arrive at superior decisions. What I believe I can provide you, however, is a way to put yourself in the best position, with the best tools, to make the best decisions at the right pace. Let me explain how the process of making better judgments and decisions begins with good listening.

I sometimes wonder if people have come to discount the value of human memory in the digital age. It seems like we view the brain's memory as analogous to computer memory—a simple storage and retrieval system for information. At the same time, instant electronic access to a virtually limitless information bank has made us somewhat complacent, perhaps even lazy. When no fact or statistic is so small or obscure that it can't be brought to appear before our eyes with just a few clicks or keystrokes, it's only to be expected that the memory muscle may start to atrophy.

Such was not the case in medieval times, as the New York University and Oxford professor Mary Carruthers makes so clear in her book, *The Book of Memory.* Carruthers holds that today when we "think of our highest creative power, we think invariably of the imagination," whereas "memory, in contrast, is devoid of intellect." She asserts that contemporary culture draws a sharp distinction between true learning and complex thought on the one hand, and rote memorization on the other. Our test of how well something has been learned is not in the recitation of the knowledge itself, but how creatively we use that knowledge in a variety of situations. According to Carruthers, ancient and medieval people would not have understood the distinction we make, for they "reserved their awe for memory." She explains that for medieval scholars, "it was memory that made knowledge into useful experience," which in turn yielded better judgment. Medieval scholars such as St. Thomas Aquinas and St. Francis of Assisi exercised and developed their memory to the point where they could recite great volumes verbatim, but that wasn't all. They valued "trained memory," that is, the ability to bring forth bits and pieces that had been learned and remembered and then mentally play with the information—take it apart and reassemble it in new ways—in order to gain new insights. A vast store of remembered information, combined with a great facility for locating and bringing up any piece of it, constituted genius.

I reach back into history to reinforce my assertion of the importance of memory because I regret how we in the modern world dismiss its contribution to superior judgment and decision making. Memory, especially as it was understood in medieval European culture, is fundamental to my approach to active listening. I try to exercise my listening muscles just as the learned souls of that era exercised their memory, to gather more and better information, and then to file that information away in a structured storage system that allows me to access everything I have learned. The "trained memory" of the medieval period is the nearest historical precedent I've encountered for my approach to purposeful listening.

Now we come to the magical part. How do we get from listening to insight? What can we do to make all that information we've gathered and filed away in our trained memory coalesce into new ideas and tangible innovation? Nobody has the answer to that question. But I do feel certain that we can increase the likelihood of such flashes of insight, and that focused listening and trained memory fertilize the ground from which new ideas spring.

Who can say why a set of facts sparks a new idea in one person and not another? The story goes that Archimedes watched the water level rise as he got into his bath and suddenly understood how to measure volume. Another tale says that Sir Isaac Newton got bonked on the head by an apple and deduced the laws of gravity. George de Mestral picked some burs out of his dog's fur after a walk in the woods and struck upon the idea for Velcro. Surely, others had experienced the very same phenomena in their lives, but without such moments of insight. What made these scientists uniquely capable of making these thrilling new connections?

Louis Pasteur famously explained the serendipitous nature of some of his own scientific discoveries this way: "Chance favors the prepared mind." Random events occur in the laboratory, but only a mind already alive with relevant facts and experience constantly colliding in a kind of mental Brownian motion will recognize the moment when the right combination of factors suddenly come together. Archimedes was already working on the problems of calculating the quantity of gold in the emperor's crown, and what came to him was a clear and elegant solution. Newton devoted a lifetime to exploring the forces that governed the mechanics of the physical universe, and his insight was a way to connect what had previously seemed to be unrelated phenomena. Mestral was a trained engineer and dedicated inventor, and when he saw how the natural hooks attached to the fur, he realized the commercial potential of adapting nature's concept. Extending this combination of analogies to its logical end, we can say that the information sorted and organized in our mental file cabinets constitutes a prepared mind. In other words, there is an indisputable connection between active, disciplined listening and fresh insights that lead to good decisions and positive action.

I've observed that the best listeners in the business environment are able to access and utilize a handful of powerful problem-solving techniques more readily and more often than their peers. First, they are acutely aware of everything that their idiosyncratic filing system already contains, or needs to contain. They move quickly to fill in the missing pieces of information, either from other areas of their stored memory or from an external source. Although they start from the assumption that everything is knowable, they do sometimes determine that a critical piece of information is not available for some reason. In such cases, they can fill in the gaps on the basis of instinct or intuition, having consciously tagged any ensuing decisions as having a greater level of risk and vulnerability because of the underlying unknowns. This allows them to feel comfortable with a certain amount of ambiguity.

Second, they rapidly shuffle and recombine any or all of the stored information, constantly adding to the options and alternatives available for consideration. If you've ever been to an eye doctor for a refraction, you'll know what I mean. The physician will test any number of lenses and prisms in front of your eyes, asking, "This one or *this* one?" refining your prescription a little bit more with each selection you make. This compare-and-contrast technique, allowing you to dismiss a progression of inferior options, makes good decisions more likely.

The philosopher Isaiah Berlin penned an essay more than fifty years ago entitled, "The Hedgehog and the Fox." In the essay, he categorized the world's greatest thinkers and philosophers as either hedgehogs—people who saw the world through the lens of a single defining idea—or foxes, who gather as much information as possible, combining and recombining it until their thinking gels into a useful insight. Dan Gardner, in his book *Future Babble: Why Expert Predictions Are Next to Worthless, and You Can Do Better*, takes Berlin one step further, arguing that the pundits and gurus of the modern world are so often wrong precisely because they function like hedgehogs. Gardner cites the research of Philip Tetlock, a professor of business and psychology who tracked the predictions of many such "experts" over twenty years, and found that those whose predictions were least accurate were the ones who adhered to an established framework of ideas, into which they tended to fit every new situation or information set. The foxes—people more comfortable with ambiguity and complexity, less invested in any cherished assumptions, and constantly hungry for new information—remained open and flexible in their thinking, and were more likely to achieve novel insights and make accurate predictions of the future. The process of comparing and contrasting allows leaders to distill the choices down until only the best options remain.

Leaders can then assess these options using a third technique, and again I will reach back into history for the most useful explanation. During the Renaissance, that explosion of intellectual and creative energy that dawned in Florence during the time of the Medicis, an intriguing exercise facilitated the pursuit of excellence in the visual arts. In Italy, in particular, when patrons or magistrates or church officials had to select an architect or artist for an important project, they occasionally employed the principle of *paragone*, which translates literally as "comparison." Works of art would be placed next to each other so that their relative merits could be weighed. Let me take you back to sixteenth-century Florence, arguably the seat of the Italian Renaissance, for an example of how it would work.

In 1503, the elder Florentine statesman Piero Soderini began seeking out artists to paint the walls of the recently completed Salone dei Cinquecento (Hall of the Five Hundred) in the city's Palazzo Vecchio. Commissions like these were common in the Italian Renaissance, when civic and religious elites acted as the primary patrons of the great masters. Soderini wanted nothing less than the best for this magnificent room. He narrowed the alternatives to two equally brilliant but uniquely talented finalists. Still, he could not choose. He decided to commission both of them: Michelangelo Buonarroti and Leonardo da Vinci. Soderini figured that if he couldn't decide which artist was the best, why not let them each complete a work and give the public the opportunity to see and admire them together? He asked the two artists to paint similar subjects—Michelangelo was to paint the fabled Battle of Cascina while Leonardo was assigned the equally important Battle of Anghiari—so that they could be compared on an apples-to-apples basis. He even gave them facing walls so that their works could be juxtaposed and contrasted.

Alas, the paintings were never completed. Leonardo's work was partially destroyed soon after he began, and Michelangelo completed only preliminary sketches before moving on to Rome, where the pope had asked him to paint the ceiling of the Sistine Chapel. Nevertheless, Soderini's approach to decision making—affording people the opportunity to appreciate and assess the work of both artists side by side—embodies this unique Renaissance practice. What makes *paragone* particularly effective in the business world is that even though it involves comparing two efforts or two proposals side by side, it is not necessarily intended to force a simple either-or decision between the two. The assumption is that each of the options has value, so the observer—that is, the decision maker—can take the best elements of each, and combine them into an entirely new option. In the best circumstances, the amalgam that results could have advantages over either of the two original options on its own.

You can think of the fourth approach to problem solving as the natural product of combining the first three techniques. The best business listeners I've observed—not coincidentally, some of the most effective business *leaders* as well—have honed their ability to call up an array of option sets at any decision point in their operation. Furthermore, they embrace the opportunity to test however many option sets are necessary before making any decisions. And they do some of this testing out loud through discussion with their colleagues. These executives understand the dangers of jumping too quickly to a point solution before test-driving all the viable alternatives. Every time I'm poised to make a big decision I remind myself of a quote by Lord D'Abernon that I read in Max Hastings's book *Winston's War*: "An Englishman's mind works best when it is almost too late."

On occasion, this process of developing and comparing options falls short of surfacing a clear favorite. In such instances, the absence of an obvious choice may indicate that for some reason, the timing isn't right for making a decision. Even in the fast-moving and fluid business environment, your first decision may be about whether or not a decision needs to be made and acted on at all or, alternatively, whether it needs to be made now or later. Delaying a decision can test the mettle of even the best of executives. Let me tell you about an experience I had with one such high-wire act. I was working with a company that generally dominated its market. This company was by far the big fellow on its block. One particular product it sold carried a high price tag and delivered a generous profit, and as evidenced by its market share, it was very popular. But times were changing, and the financial pressures on the firm's customers were increasing. At the same time, the company was developing technologies for a product that would be significantly cheaper to produce. It had made this advancement to prepare for price-conscious new customers in emerging markets. The company faced a critical decision. On the one hand, it could choose to introduce the much lower-cost, lower-priced machine into the home market as well as the emerging ones. Doing so would introduce the risk of cannibalizing the current (high-priced) installed base, but it could also end up expanding the entire market. On the other hand, the company weighed the option of not offering the lower-priced machine to the home market at all. The risk of delay was that it created a window of opportunity for the company's competitors to jump into the market with a similar low-priced product of their own.

My client thought long and hard about the decision, and specifically focused on the timing. Eventually the company postponed the decision to a specific date on which it would consider entering the mature market with its low-priced product. In the end, the company did decide to enter but did so just ahead of competitors. How did this story play out? It's still too early to tell, but the decision to postpone could only have been reached through a disciplined process that was informed by listening well in the marketplace. This company maintained close and constant communications with its customers and its suppliers, both of which groups were able to share important information that contained clues to the competition's plans. The company further probed its customers about how the lower-priced product might change their purchasing and usage patterns. It learned that the lower price could actually induce customers to buy more units, triggering an expansion of the market.

It's worth looking at these various approaches and historical paradigms in combination, and using them together as you would in actual practice. Let's imagine that you are in charge of a construction project, perhaps a public building, at the earliest stages of architectural design. Architecture seems to occupy a unique position at the intersection of form and function, of aesthetics and practicality.

In the first phase of the process, you listen to all the relevant parties, gathering the information that will fill your file folders of Mandate, Plan, Team, and so forth. You ask the questions that allow you to determine functional priorities, commitments to stakeholders, traffic flow, community involvement, adaptability, suitability to the neighborhood—anything that might be a consideration in design, construction and operation.

Next you begin to assemble the important bits of information into as many different combinations as possible. This is the moment at which a vast array of *inputs* is converted into a limited number of select *outputs*. In the case of a multipurpose public building, there are a daunting number of possible permutations related to usage alone. Then come the particulars of design and materials, where each decision will have an impact on the use and comfort and safety and experience of the building. The architectural team, at this point, can be literally putting the various pieces of the building together dozens or hundreds of times in as many different ways, with each new output either demonstrating why some alternative component should be discarded, or suggesting the addition of other possible alternatives. We've come a long way from the meticulous hand-wrought schematics of the Middle Ages or even the Renaissance to today's computer-aided design programs that allow you to swap out multiple elements with the press of a button.

At the end of this process, you might end up with several, or perhaps just two, best options from which to choose—complete proposals that each, in their own way, satisfy all the requirements of the project. These can then be held up for scrutiny and comparison, according to the *paragone* model. And remember that the final decision is not a simple either-or choice. The beauty of the *paragone* process is the presumption that each of the options has value, so that the choice might ultimately entail using elements of all the proposals, but none of them in their entirety.

It is nearly impossible to define or explain the precise moment at which good listening is transformed into better judgment, but I've tried to provide you with the blueprint for incorporating good listening into an efficient and reliable process for assessing options, weighing risks, and making well-informed decisions. We've talked about listening, probing, collecting, and filing—in short, the ways in which we inform a trained memory to know what we have in the file drawers. Although there is no step-by-step manual for transforming that base of knowledge and experience into better thinking, what I can tell you is that if you don't get at least this far, you have less chance of success.

The Harvard business professor Clayton Christensen reminds us that coming up with good insights is the essential job of every leader, wherever he or she may fall on the organizational chart, and that the skills to produce those insights must be honed and nurtured through consistent practice. He goes further to say that "the most important skill to practice is questioning," and as we know, questioning is the first prerequisite for good listening. Christensen advises leaders never to stop asking "Why?" and "Why not?" "Ask questions that both impose and eliminate constraints," he writes. "This will help you see a problem or opportunity from a different angle."

That different angle may present the perfect refraction that sparks the fresh insight that leads to a good decision.

Changing Your Organization
through Listening

One of the themes that I have rehearsed throughout this book has been the idea that good listening is a key driver of high individual performance. I have argued that how well a manager performs in an organization is determined by the kinds of decisions that he makes, which in turn are based on how well he listens. In the end, better performance is always the ultimate goal. In this chapter, I want to talk about a different kind of performance, because I believe that not only can the quality of your listening determine your own *individual* performance, but it can also shape that of your *organization*.

An organization's performance is driven by a wide array of disparate factors. However, one of the most essential ingredients is also one of the most resistant to definition—an organization's *culture*. This term has been used so often that it has lost much of its meaning. Even the countless experts on organizational culture have a hard time defining the term. Yet there does seem to be some agreement that a company's culture is made up of the constellation of values, aspirations, rules, measures, and expectations that shape the activities of its members.

Think about the difference between a stereotypical Silicon Valley start-up and a Wall Street investment bank. The start-up's employees come to work every day in T-shirts, jeans, and flip-flops. They work in an open room where collaboration and engagement are not only encouraged, but expected. Their success is judged less by how well they execute than by how many new ideas they generate. And when their company grows too big, many of them will bail out and join a new start-up venture. The investment bank, on the other hand, is populated by buttoned-up, suit-wearing Ivy Leaguers. They work long hours and are judged primarily on how quickly and effectively they can process large amounts of information and develop clear analytical insights. Success for them will mean rising fast through the company to positions of greater responsibility. Clearly, these are two different models, with two entirely different cultures—both successful in their own ways and for their own purposes. Each one provides its members with a set of unspoken guidelines for how they are expected to conduct themselves, as well as how they are expected to perform.

Because it influences the performance of each individual, a business's culture is critical in determining how well a business performs in the collective. Yet what is culture actually built on? How does it evolve within an organization? It seems to me that, at its essence, a corporation's culture is really the sum of all the many hundreds and thousands of personal interactions between its members. Face-to-face conversations, discussions, presentations, debates, and meetings— these are the building blocks of culture.

I think by now you can see where I'm going with this. Though cultures evolve organically more often than by design, there is no doubt that they are shaped in large part by company leaders.

Managers set the standards within their organizations through their interactions with others. They use their conversations and discussions as tools, not only to better their own performance, but also to lead by example, to demonstrate what they believe to be, or what they would wish to be, the acceptable norms and boundaries for behavior and performance. In an ideal world, individuals lower down the corporate ladder will emulate the leaders' behavior and bring the same practices into their own interactions. Eventually, as these attitudes and behaviors radiate throughout the organization, culture takes shape. That's not always a good thing, mind you. A leader's example is followed regardless of whether it's good or bad. Many a company has foundered because of less-than-constructive behaviors by the people at, or rising to, the top.

I once had occasion to discuss this topic with a general in the U.S. Marine Corps. He credited the lieutenants and captains in his division for setting the culture. He believed that if these officers consistently behaved according to a high standard, it was possible to build a very high-performing unit that could accomplish great things under the worst of circumstances. Funnily enough, when I followed up with the lieutenants, they echoed the general's sentiment, only with a twist: they believed it was the sergeants who made the difference in the divisional culture. Although the personnel at each level deferred to the next level down in that hierarchy, it was clear to me that the important behavioral cues that set the tone for the division were coming from above. This included the modesty that allowed them all to credit the people below them. At each level of command, it was understood that a responsibility existed to model the behavior expected of leaders throughout the hierarchy, if the unit was to have any hope of performing to its full potential.

Good listening means having productive and respectful interactions. I have described many techniques for achieving this level of listening proficiency. Until now, these listening skills have always been about helping you. You will find, however, that as you listen better and your interactions with colleagues improve you will actually begin to affect the behaviors of those around you and the culture of the organization or unit that you manage. Kevin Sharer, the CEO of Amgen, told me, "When I began as a chief executive officer I thought my job was to exercise power and drive outcomes. How wrong I was. I learned that my job was to architect the environment to listen." It's absolutely true; when that particular attitude ripples throughout an organization, the effects can be profound. Let's explore how, through good listening, you will make positive cultural change happen in your business.

Foster a more disciplined and productive organization.

Think about what better listening skills can do for one-on-one conversations. These techniques should make for more efficient and more complete communication, in which no information is withheld, and all ideas and perspectives are surfaced. This means less time wasted rehashing issues. It means getting to decisions that are better informed and more thoroughly reasoned, and getting to those decisions at the right time.

If better listening can have that effect on individual interactions, imagine the impact on broader-scale communications. I'm talking about a great deal more than more useful and productive meetings. Recall that CEO I described, who was dissatisfied with the interactions and decision-making processes in his financial services company. He responded by instituting a carefully constructed weekly global telephone conference, with a concrete agenda and strict requirements for preparation and information gathering. This weekly listening forum unified the multiple agendas and calendars throughout far-flung elements of the company, sharpened the collective focus of his team, and solidified their purpose. But even more than that, the effect on the corporate culture of practical steps like this weekly teleconference was like clearing a logjam in a mountain stream. It allowed the techniques and approaches favored by the CEO to spread through the entire company. He demanded that his team come to the meeting consistently prepared with both information and analysis, which required them to be more organized and disciplined in gathering the necessary data from their own departments. In this way, the heightened attention to better practice cascaded down throughout the company, imprinting the leader's own disciplined listening on the entire organization.

The final thing to keep in mind here is that discipline in an organization, and the efficiency and productivity that flow from it, require a shared understanding that deliberation must lead to decision and action. One of the funniest encounters I've witnessed happened between two members of a team who were sitting around a table discussing how to forge ahead with a complicated market-entry strategy. They were on the precipice of a decision when one of the individuals had a radical idea about how to overhaul the entire approach, but he was having an extremely difficult time expressing it. His explanation rambled along, as he thought out loud refining "on the fly" an idea that had clearly not been fully formed in his head. Finally the team leader jumped in: "Okay, Jim, time to land the plane!" he said. Everyone laughed, including the man who'd been talking. The comment snapped him out of his rambling meditation like the crack of a whip. He and the rest of the team knew, on the basis of their past experiences with each other, that even good ideas had to come down to a point that would ultimately lead to action. The team leader was reinforcing this shared understanding with his comment. It showed me that when directed and purposeful conversations are the rule, team members will generally develop an instinctive awareness of how much discussion is enough. They know what every conversation is meant to achieve, and exactly what information they need to get to that goal. In that kind of culture, leaders can safely say when they've heard enough, without fear of communicating any disrespect.

Ensure the free and open flow of information and ideas.

I was amused when John McLaughlin, the CIA deputy, told me that when he had to make a tough decision he ended his conversations with his colleagues with this question: "Is there anything left that you haven't told me . . . because I don't want you to leave this room and go down the hall to your buddy's office and tell him that I just didn't get it." With that question McLaughlin would communicate three things: he established the expectation that his colleagues should be prepared; he demanded that everything come out onto the table; and he signaled his respect for what his CPs had to say. There was no room for coasting with McLaughlin. You were expected to have new ideas, to state them often, and to state them clearly. You also had to be ready to respond to his incessant probing and questioning. Great leaders, with their constant challenging, get the best out of their CPs, raise the bar, and create an exciting and productive environment. The net result is that communication becomes more thoughtful, more complete, and much more dynamic.

I'm sure you've had conversations in which you nodded politely at whatever your CP was saying, in the manner of a Pretender, but either returned quickly to what you were saying or moved on to another topic altogether when he was finished. A few carefully chosen questions to your CP would have let him know that you had been paying attention—that you had been listening. Instead, your pretending indicated only that it wasn't worth your CPs time or effort to try to communicate any information. Any type of poor listener, whether it's the Pretender, the Opinionator, or the Answer Man, can have the same kind of stultifying effect on workplace communication. If people believe that their contributions don't matter, they will eventually simply stop offering them. It isn't necessary that you agree with or act on what your CP says. The knowledge that you are listening engenders mutual trust and respect, which in the end are the key ingredients of a culture that thrives on the free and open flow of information and ideas.

Establish a reverence for fact-based discussions.

I'll never forget sitting in a meeting of a company's top management team, in which the acquisition of another company was under consideration. In the middle of the debate, one of the executives jumped in, having made up his mind. He explained to the group that the acquisition would be a mistake for them. When he was done, the CEO gave him a hard look and said, "Is that opinion, or is that fact?" The executive was a bit taken aback, and didn't respond immediately. "Because what I need now," the CEO continued, "is fact. More facts."

It sounds like the CEO was cutting off discussion, which a good listener does not want to do, but the opposite is true. The CEO was certainly cutting off that executive—and none too tactfully—but his goal was to keep the conversation going. He saw that his colleague had tried to close the discussion prematurely, before all the necessary facts had been gathered, and before the real work of asking questions and refining the information had begun in earnest.

A culture that treasures good information rewards the effort to test and challenge both facts and assumptions until they are either confirmed or discarded. It takes concentrated effort, and perhaps even a formalized procedural framework, to step back from whatever issue may be on the table in front of us and ask some basic questions: What are the assumptions underlying this discussion, and do they hold water? Many of our assumptions may be perfectly valid, but until we purposefully ask the question, and prove them to be one way or the other, they will always remain things we assume, instead of things we *know*. Unproven assumptions are insidious, as we tend to distort what we hear so that it conforms to what we already believe.

In a good-information culture, people develop confidence in the information with which they work. Furthermore, if you are confident of the process that qualifies the information, it allows you to live with uncertainty and ambiguity. Not every fact can be ascertained; not every assumption can be proved or disproved, but you can only be comfortable with those situations if you know that every effort has been made to make a determination. Only then can you live comfortably with uncertainties in your decision-making process.

Generate new insights and more creative solutions.

Leaders who consistently look for new approaches to decision making, who seek as many relevant perspectives on an issue as possible, encourage people to tackle new problems in the same way. A leader who consistently demonstrates the thinking of a fox, as opposed to that of a hedgehog, empowers the entire organization to function similarly. Individuals and organizations that can gather, sort, retrieve, and manipulate vast quantities of reliable information with ease and fluidity are capable of running every question or problem through a multiplicity of refractions and developing a complete spectrum of alternative answers and solutions. Remember all the creative techniques handed down to us through history, from the medieval memory masters to the Renaissance ideal of *paragone*. These are the processes that expand understanding, and that create fertile ground for fresh insight, creative problem solving, and, from time to time, genuine innovation.

Mark Little, who is a senior vice president at General Electric and the head of the company's global research center, explained in an interview to *McKinsey Quarterly* how GE uses techniques like comparison and *paragone* to boost their researchers' creativity and improve the quality of their ideas. On the one hand, he says, there is the philosophy of "we are sisterhood, we are brotherhood, we are collaboration, we are teamwork." Yet on the other hand, GE combines this collegiality with the practice of productive rivalry; one team is asked to look at a problem one way, another team another way, and then the two come together to compare notes and see how the two solutions can be wedded into something even better. "Rivalry takes place in an atmosphere of trying to produce results together . . . Some guys look at A; some guys look at B. You tell us all about A; you tell us all about B. And then we'll sort it out. Whether A or B wins, these teams will come together to make it a success." He says that GE has used these techniques to achieve more creative insights on countless technologies, from aircraft engines, to solar panels, to power generation. In this sense, GE replicates the same processes of recombining information, looking at it in new ways, and comparing different approaches and solutions that I advocated when discussing how to connect listening to judgment. What's more, they are able to do this across the entire organization.

Build an organization that excites and energizes its people.

Earlier in my career, I admired a colleague who held a stressful administrative position in which he was responsible for leading the activities of an office full of hard-charging professionals operating in a highly competitive environment. It would have been easy for him to become cynical or to burn out under the avalanche of issues that fell across his desk each morning. Instead, he seemed to relish every new problem, no matter how dire or unexpected it may have been, and never looked on such difficulties as "bumps in the road." "This *is* the road," he would insist. "If stuff like this didn't happen, they wouldn't need people like me in these jobs!" For him, this was when the fun started, when he got to test himself, and with luck, experience the satisfaction of clearing another hurdle. And he was never happier than when he was surrounded by colleagues who responded to challenges in the same way.

Organizations that value creativity, reward debate, respect dissent, and celebrate breakthrough insights are extremely attractive to talented individuals. The basis for all these positive characteristics lies in the interpersonal interactions that shape the culture of the organization, and the quality of those interactions is invariably rooted in good listening. Such organizations are more likely to respond thoughtfully, yet aggressively, to challenges. They will have institutionalized processes that allow them to quickly identify the available decision-making options, and to determine what information is required in order to make those decisions. These organizations will relish the opportunity to examine a new problem from multiple perspectives, and experiment with multiple solutions.

What to Do on Monday Morning

I don't sing very well. It's a struggle for me just to get through "The Star-Spangled Banner" at a sporting event. I can scarcely imagine how overwhelming it must be for an opera singer embarking on a new role. She has to master the notes and study the dynamics, while also memorizing the lyrics, often in a language that's not her own. And on top of all that, she has to act the scenes, learning her cues and her blocking. Then, of course, there is the recreational golfer who decides to take a few lessons and improve his game. The first time he steps up to the tee after a few sessions, his head is so cluttered with thoughts about his stance, his grip, the angles of his knees and elbows, that he's all but paralyzed.

It would be understandable if you felt this way about listening after everything I've given you to think about here. I've discussed how to get the information from your conversation partners that you need to make better business decisions. I've outlined ways to sort, store, retrieve, and use that information to gain new insights and develop new ideas. I've described how you can model your listening behaviors to shape a more productive organizational culture. It's an awful lot to keep in mind, so I'll close with the same advice that any good teacher in any complex discipline will offer: Don't try to do it all at once. Practice one thing at a time, over and over again, then move to the next, and soon you will feel it begin to come together. A great diva will get an aria down cold before she starts worrying about the stagecraft. A savvy golfer will take as many swings as needed to get his rhythm and tempo consistent before moving on to target lines and trajectories.

Listening is no different. I said at the outset that listening is a skill you can learn by breaking it down into its component parts, and then incorporating each aspect one at a time. Once that practice becomes second nature, you can move on to the next part. The good news is that it will be a lot easier to master the techniques of good listening than it would be to make your way to the stage of the Metropolitan Opera or the clubhouse at the Masters. I've traveled that road to becoming a better listener—and in turn a better business problem solver and decision maker. I am still on that journey. So I thought that I would leave you with a list of things to begin doing on Monday morning. It is a list that has served me well and one that continues to remind me of what I must aspire to master.

1. Keep quiet.

The more you're talking, the less you're listening. Watch yourself for any telltale behaviors of the classic poor listening types, like the Opinionator, the Perseverator, or the Answer Man, and do your best to nip those in the bud. Never lose sight of the first priority of conversation: to gather information. Your goal is to cede the lion's share of the airtime to your conversation partner. Let the 80/20 rule be your gold standard, with your CP talking 80 percent of the time. When you do speak, you want to be asking, not telling—probe and question in order to bring out everything your CP might have to offer. Use your questions to clarify and to expand, to fill in details, to shed light on opposing perspectives, and to enable your CP to explore new avenues of thought that can lead to unexpected insights.

It almost goes without saying that even the best listener requires conversation partners who want to share. I've made the point that listening is the responsibility of any leader or manager. At the same time, however, your CP has an equal responsibility to leave nothing unsaid, but that responsibility should never feel like a burden. In a business environment that values all constructive communication, people will feel eager to contribute, excited by the opportunity to raise their game and that of the entire organization. A productive organizational culture rests on a foundation of interpersonal trust and respect. Each individual must feel confident that he or she will be heard, and that any and all ideas can be put on the table without fear of penalty or scorn.

2. Challenge assumptions.

Entrenched assumptions are pure poison to effective decision making. Anything you take for granted, without first stopping to question, investigate, and confirm, establishes an artificial boundary on productive problem solving. Both you and your CP need to enter into a dialogue with a mutual understanding of any underlying assumptions, and with an open exchange about whether or not those assumptions have been tested, and how much weight they carry. This is where the questioner's art is perhaps most important. If you have become the Master of the Question, this is where you show your stuff, by asking the simple, fundamental questions: How do we know that? Why do we think that? Can we prove that?

3. Focus on what you need to know.

In an organizational culture that values active, focused listening, all the participants share an understanding of the purpose of an interaction. Enter into conversations knowing either what information you need to collect—which file folders are to be filled—or what you should be prepared to communicate. Great listening means minimizing the inevitable detours and digressions and distractions, so that time and effort are maximized.

4. Increase your tolerance for ambiguity and uncertainty.

Yes, you listen in order to gather information, and I hope you will use the techniques in this book to ensure that the information is as complete and reliable as possible. In reality, however, some decisions you face will demand information that simply doesn't exist, or is for some reason suspect or fragmented. Remember John McLaughlin's description of the unpredictable flow of imperfect and ambiguous information on which the CIA was constantly forced to base critical decisions. If you are used to challenging and qualifying information as a matter of course, you will be able to identify and isolate the areas of uncertainty. When you know what you don't know, you can incorporate flexibility into your planning by creating a set of contingencies that can kick in as information becomes more available and concrete.

5. Sort incoming information into the appropriate file drawers and folders.

This is the system that works for me. My imaginary filing system, which encompasses everything from Mandate to Personal, makes it possible for me to maintain control over the masses of information that come at me every day in business, and that inform even the most minor decisions. Maybe your business necessitates a different list of categories, or maybe the filing metaphor doesn't work for you. It doesn't matter. You need a system to organize the ever-swelling tide of information that washes over a good listener. "Information over-load" is no joke; if your improved listening skills bring you no other benefit than reducing the noise and panic brought on by information bombardment, then I've accomplished something worthwhile.

6. Work your memory to gain insights.

This is why it's so critical to sort and store information: to have ready access to it when the time comes to move from conversation to action. It's one thing to have an abundance of data at your disposal. It's quite another to put it to work for you, as the fuel that powers creative problem solving and effective decision making. Recall that medieval scholars didn't necessarily distinguish between great feats of memorization and the abstractions of intellectual thought. It is the pairing of these two cognitive processes that gives birth to true insight. I've described a number of different techniques for identifying the relevant information in a situation, then disassembling and reassembling that fact set in as many different ways as are necessary to produce new ideas and insights. If you know of other approaches, or have devised your own, that's great, as long as your goal is to consistently get the best options on the table so you and your team can make the best decisions.

7. Know when to pull the trigger.

Sounds simple, right? It is, when you are listening with purpose and with focus. It's my belief that if the goal or intent of a conversation is clear in your mind at the outset, you'll know intuitively when it's time to transition from debate to action. Sometimes you'll have no choice; you'll have to act immediately. Nonetheless, you'll know which of your mental file drawers are relevant and complete. Knowing when to pull the trigger may be the most delicate component of good listening. You train yourself to take it all in, to leave no stone unturned, to give everyone a say, and to probe relentlessly. It feels somehow strange to put up a hand and declare, "Okay, we're done. It's time to act." And yet, getting to action is the whole point. Efficiency and productivity and positive forward motion depend on it. Listening never stops, but you need to know when to close the debate and push forward.

8. Demonstrate the best listening practices to lift everyone's game.

In the previous chapter, I made the point that organizations tend to emulate the practices of their leaders, and that if a leader is able to model the behavior of a great listener, all kinds of benefits are likely to accrue to the organization. Good listeners are thoughtful, yet open to spontaneous insight; they question and challenge without mercy, but are also more than willing to give any individual or any idea due consideration; they are deliberate but not dilatory. It strikes me that these are the very same qualities to which any organization aspires, and that if enough individuals can adopt some of these behaviors, it won't be long before they become the hallmarks of an organization's culture.

• • •

Don't expect a tin ear to evolve into a platinum one overnight. It takes time, discipline, and constant attention. In my conversation with Kevin Sharer, he recalled being a junior officer in the Navy's submarine fleet. He explained that he was young, ambitious, and a less-than-stellar listener. Sharer believes that many people, especially early in their careers, tend to approach conversations already believing that they are smarter than their CP, and consumed by the need to convey their opinion and prove their smarts. Kevin told me that later in life, he took the extraordinary step of seeking out his former submarine commander so that he could apologize for having been such a poor listener.

Most of us probably have a list of people to whom we'd like to apologize for our previous listening sins, but Sharer's story got me wondering how much knowledge and insight we have all missed out on because our listening skills weren't up to snuff. My final message is this: There's no time like the present. Start your new listening journey right now, by trying to substitute one good listening practice that seems most natural to you for one bad one that you have identified. As with so many efforts at self-improvement, half the battle is already won the moment you make the decision to try and the commitment to apply yourself. I hope you're excited by the prospect of the fuller and richer world that good listening can open up for you. I know I am.

INDEX

Emotions
  as distractions, 70–73, 71
  emotionless silence, value of, 44
End of discussion. *See* Closing
  conversation
Engel, George, 30
Excitement
  as distraction, 72
  organizational, creating, 172–73
Execution, 7, 123–34
  complexity, managing, 128–29
  and decision making process, 124–26
  elements of, 123–24
  good execution, example of, 131–34
  and information flow, 127–28
  rhythm of, 129–31

Facts, discussions based on, 169–70
False consensus, 58
Financial crisis (2008), 59, 61
Fixation on ideas, by Perseverators, 22–23
Focus. *See* Attention/focus

Gardner, Dan, 157
General Electric, 118, 171
Grouch, listening problem of, 20

Harvey, Jerry, 100–101
Hastings, Max, 159
Hedonic adaptation, 58
Herding instinct, 58–59
Hippocratic Oath, 18
Holmes, Sherlock, 55–56
Hunter, Holly, 45

IBM, 94
Impatience, and interrupting, 46, 71
Impressing others
  by Answer Man, 23–24
  by interrupting, 46
Individual differences
  and learning listening skills, 4–5
  of medical patients, 31
  respect for, 34–35

Information, filing system
  execution, 7, 123–34
  functions of, 82–84, 179
  mandate, 7, 87–96
  personal, 7, 135–46
  personal preferences for, 83–84
  plan, 7, 97–109
  team, 7, 110–22
Information overload
  avoiding, 49
  impact on communication, 46
Initiatives
  to achieve objectives, 102–3
  litmus test for, 103
Insight
  path to, 154–62
  See also Decision making; Problem
  solving
Intangible assets, 104–5
Interruptions
  breaking silence, timing for, 44–50
  controlling, method for, 46–48
  and impatience, 46, 71
  by Opinionator, 19

Judgment. *See* Decision making

Kaplan, Steven, 43
Kipling, Rudyard, 50–51
Klebanov, Mark, 43
Koch, Ed, 32
Kurosawa, Akira, 139–40

Leaders/leadership
  burn-out, 16
  challenges to, 15
  compartmentalizing by, 69–70
  good listening, benefits from, 41, 48–49
  managerial rhythm, 129–31
  and organizational culture, 164–65, 167
  popularity and listening ability, 41, 48
  showmanship, negative aspects, 43
  success, traits related to, 43